KEEP YOUR PAYCHECK, LIVE YOUR PASSION

How to fulfill your dream without having to quit your day job

Erika Welz Prafder
with Carole Sovocool

Adams Media
Avon, Massachusetts

To Dwight,
You healed my heart.

Published by Adams Media, an F+W Publications Company
57 Littlefield Street, Avon, MA 02322
www.adamsmedia.com

ISBN: 1-59337-264-7
Printed in Canada.
J I H G F E D C B A

Library of Congress Cataloging-in-Publication Data
Prafder, Erika Welz.
Keep your paycheck, live your passion / Erika Welz Prafder
with Carole Sovocool.
p.   cm.
ISBN 1-59337-264-7
1. Success in business. 2. New business enterprises. 3. Career development. 4.
Job hunting. I. Sovocool, Carole. II. Title.

HF5386.P82 2005
650.1--dc22

2004026358

This publication is designed to provide accurate and authoritative information with
regard to the subject matter covered. It is sold with the understanding that the publisher is not engaged in rendering legal, accounting, or other professional advice. If
legal advice or other expert assistance is required, the services of a competent professional person should be sought.

—From a *Declaration of Principles* jointly adopted by a Committee of the
American Bar Association and a Committee of Publishers and Associations

Many of the designations used by manufacturers and sellers to distinguish their
products are claimed as trademarks. Where those designations appear in this book
and Adams Media was aware of a trademark claim, the designations have been
printed with initial capital letters.

This book is available at quantity discounts for bulk purchases.
For information, please call 1-800-872-5627.

Acknowledgments

I n the fall of 2003, I embarked on two creative processes: writing this book and beginning a high-risk pregnancy. At the advice of my cardiologist, Dr. Narendra Hadpawat, I had "faith, not fear" that I'd successfully complete both works. To him and the outstanding team of doctors who cared for me, I am eternally grateful.

To Roy and Leah Neuberger, Rebbetzin Esther Jungreis, and Rabbi Danny and Bonnie Frankel—Bless you for being a source of hope and spiritual guidance in my time of need.

I'd like to thank *The New York Post* for paying me to chat with and write about people of such incredible vision and perseverance over the years. It's not just a cool job, it's an education and treat.

Respect to Jill Alexander, a talented editor and "evolved" soul at Adams Media. Cheers to you for instantly recognizing the merit of our book idea and for lobbying your powers-that-be to give it the green light.

Special thanks to my legal advisor, Stephen Moelis, whose seamless expertise allowed me to confidently sign on to this project.

It's my good fortune to have such a gifted and devoted writing partner. Carole, your upbeat attitude and "editing magic" truly elevated this book. You are as sincere as you are witty and a pleasure to collaborate with.

Without the encouragement and reassurance of my immediate and extended families, I wouldn't have made this manuscript's deadline. You can't put a price tag on support like that.

Creative types need inspiration and purpose to keep their passion alive. My wonderful husband is a never-ending source of both. I love you, Richie. Thanks for believing in me and in the promise of our precious little miracle.

—*Erika Welz Prafder*

Introduction

J ust as there is an art to flexing one's creativity, there is also an art to creating cash flow. Unfortunately, trying to succeed at both is tricky—especially if you want to eat. But it *can* and *has* been done. That's what this book is all about.

When I started out in the work world, I wasn't aware of this fact. Miserable and restless at my $50K-a-year job in Internet marketing, I felt I should stick things out. After all, I was a twenty-three-year-old college graduate. It was time to buckle down and put my degree to use—especially with my name on the apartment lease and the utility bills.

Although I'd always sensed I was destined for entrepreneurship, no idea for a business had yet come to light. Any thoughts of working for myself still seemed dreadfully far-fetched.

But as fate had it, in 1995 I met my future husband, a self-made businessman and a talented saxophonist. He opened my eyes as no college professor, headhunter, or well-meaning relative had before. Here was a guy who was living his passion, and living *off of it* as well. He spent six months a year operating a swimming pool company and the other half touring and making CDs. As a creative person, he understood that time and flexibility are precious commodities, and he had devised a way to have plenty of both in order to pursue his pleasures.

That's all it took for me—seeing living proof of a *different* way to a more inspired, enjoyable life. Over the next decade, rather than being so rational and preplanned, I tried to be more intuitive. Instead of adhering to an expected career norm, I chose to follow only those interests that stemmed from my heart. As I surrendered to my inner compass, soon enough I honed in on something I'd long believed there was a need for—helping to steer young people on to their ideal career paths.

So, while still holding down a full-time position, I spent the wee hours of my nights and many long weekends thinking, planning, and ultimately launching an internship placement agency for college students. Not only did I earn enough income to relinquish my day job, but this first-of-its-kind business endeavor opened up new doors for me as a career advice columnist and—now—book author.

While wearing my writer's hat, I've had the pleasure of interviewing true heroes in American business today. This cross section of talent stretches from a yuppie-turned-yoga teacher to a mom/jewelry designer, to a traveling photographer of musicians and a secretary by day/crochet artist by night. Unwilling to settle for a mediocre existence, these folks bucked the traditional nine-to-five system, and they have all found ways to profit from their own special gifts.

I've shared many of their motivating stories in the chapters that follow. In addition, there's plenty of useful information and expert advice on today's hottest business niches, how to sell your idea, and the most creative occupations.

We've even picked the brains of some of the business world's most creative top guns. They reveal their secrets for hitting it big. As you'll discover, passion doesn't come cheap. You may need to work two jobs, endure rejection, return to school, relocate, or invest every last dime you have in order to turn your creative vision into money.

You'll undoubtedly work harder for yourself than you ever did for someone else. But isn't your happiness worth the sacrifice? If you've decided to bet on yourself, this book is for you. Writing it was a product of my creative freedom, and reading it just may be the kick start you need for your own. So read on. Begin working on your labor of love—and go get paid!

—Erika Welz Prafder
(Please send correspondence to
P.O. Box 235
Atlantic Beach, NY 11509
or *ewprafder@optonline.net*

Chapter 1

Dream a Little Dream:
Finding What You Really Love to Do

I f you were to go to an elementary school and pick a random selection of children, very few would tell you that they want to become bank tellers, insurance agents, or retail salespeople. Most have lofty ambitions—actor, writer, pop star.

Yet very few of them realize their dreams. Some will pursue them, only to find that either through bad luck or lack of resolve they are not destined to become the next big thing. Some will never have the encouragement or right opportunities. They'll lack the right mentor or access to further education. Eventually, most of them will give up on pursuing a career that they find emotionally and intellectually fulfilling.

Others will find that, as their life progresses, other skills come to the forefront and dictate their careers. Either way, somewhere along the line, reality bites. And hard. Life's demands begin piling up, and soon there are bills to be paid each month and commitments to be met. The job that was taken as an interim gig becomes permanent.

For some, a hobby can fulfill the need for creative expression or an entrepreneurial outlet. Evening and weekend opportunities abound for the dabbler. But for many, the longing is not just to be involved in these extracurriculars, but to excel at them. The artist wants to show his work. The dancer wants to perform. The actor wants to be captured on celluloid.

1

Can you throw everything up in the air and hunt this buried treasure? Can you quit your job, cash in your employee stock plan, and attempt to live the dream? Quite honestly—the answer is probably not, simply because you may be past the point of no return (see any forty-somethings on *American Idol*?), or you're too used to your standard of living to revert to eating macaroni and cheese dinners and living with six roommates. So what is the answer? To coexist. Having two successful careers side by side is not impossible. It's simply a question of determination, time management, and inspiration.

I'm a Believer

First of all, if you don't believe in yourself, your talent, your dreams, then forget about it. The person who believes has no questions. The person who does not believe has no answers. The alternative to not keeping your creativity alive is to have your soul slowly disintegrate with time. It may take a fair amount of soul searching to identify the obstacles that prevent you from realizing your dreams. Some people coast through life with one finger on the snooze button. It takes less work to suppress your innermost creative aspirations and dreams than it does to respond to a wake-up call from your heart.

Often, the anxiety and discontentment we feel in our work lives stem from our failure to recognize the real sources of the messages that influence our decisions, according to Dr. Dorothy Cantor, a practicing psychologist from Westfield, New Jersey. "We need to be aware of the voices that lead us in a particular direction and ask ourselves if it serves us and reflects who we really are," she explained.

For example, perhaps you've questioned your choice to return to work after your child was born. Where is this insecurity coming from? Do you really want to be a stay-at-home mom, or do you feel pressured by the disapproving opinion of some child-care experts, friends, family, or colleagues, who caution that the first years of a child's life are critical to his emotional/psychological development and therefore you'd better stick around?

Living the Dream

Wells Jenkins, creator, Wells-Ware

For Wells Jenkins, having big dreams paid off literally overnight. After years as an architect who designed hospitals and medical facilities, the young, Manhattan-based career woman envisioned the product that would change her fate while she was asleep.

"I saw this necklace," she said. "It had charms of my childhood on it, filled with family photographs, old postcards, and keepsakes. It was my life miniaturized." The following day, Wells trekked down to Canal Street in pursuit of a metal welder. "I found a street vendor who agreed to teach me how to weld if I bought his tools," she recalled.

Able to craft her necklace from memory, Wells sported her new possession while walking the city streets. She received so much praise and inquiries from passersby that she called up Barneys, the renowned upscale department store, to feel out their interest. "They asked me to come in that day and immediately placed a large order," she said.

Since that first sale in 1991, the Wells-Ware jewelry line has expanded to include cufflinks, earrings, bracelets, corporate gifts, and made-to-order pieces. The company mailing list exceeds 20,000 people, and some of her clients top the entertainment industry's list of who's who, including Julia Roberts, Sting, Meredith Viera, and Oprah Winfrey.

Taking the time to analyze your inner voice can lead to new revelations about what job you should have or whether you should work at all, and plus you'll save a bundle in career or psychological counseling! Hopefully, "you'll find a greater degree of confidence and satisfaction in the choices you do elect," said Dr. Cantor.

While You Were Sleeping

Do you have recurring sweet dreams or frightening nightmares? Do the images and themes evoke feelings of terror and anxiety? In your dreams are you fantasizing about a life you aren't living in your waking state? Well then, take note! There is much to be learned from these night stories. By interpreting the messages you receive in your sleep state, you can uncover what you may really be yearning for in your work life, according to Veronica Tonay, Ph.D., a practicing psychologist, dream expert, and author based in Santa Cruz, California.

"I sometimes dream of a favorite serene spot in London. In my dream, I'm upset because I only have just one day to enjoy myself before catching a plane home. I usually have this dream when I'm overworked and need to stop and smell the roses," said Dr. Tonay.

Each of us dreams an average of five times a night, but creative types tend to remember the experience more often. Experts assert that we basically behave in our dreams as we do in waking life. So, if you're experiencing apprehension or dissatisfaction at work, you may fantasize about arguing with your boss, missing a deadline, being late, or, if you're feeling vulnerable, having to give a presentation wearing absolutely nothing.

Do you dream of flying during your slumbered state? "Flying symbolizes freedom and joy. You may be running low on these," said Dr. Tonay. Sexual dreams are rarely about lust. Rather, Dr. Tonay said, "They expose traits that you lack and want for yourself. Such qualities include power, control, a free spirit, or confidence." If you're running for your life or jumping off of a cliff in your dreams, "Perhaps you're about to make a transition or take a huge risk and have a fear of failing," advised Dr. Tonay.

One of Tonay's clients repeatedly dreamed of lovely homes alongside a stream. She sensed some kind of change happening in these houses. "In her real life, she was an unhappy, unchallenged secretary who wanted to break into real estate. Two years later, she was earning

$200,000 a year from her successful new career," said Dr. Tonay. Having examined more than 20,000 dreams, Tonay claims the first step in analyzing dreams is paying attention.

"Keep a two-week diary of your dreams. The payoff may be a better understanding of yourself, stimulating your creative side and enhancing your relationships." You may also find some clues about what it is you really want to be doing creatively or professionally.

If you can't easily recall your nocturnal visions, ask yourself why. Be sure to rule out any fear or intimidation. As frightening as it may sound, even nightmares are a good thing, said Dr. Tonay. "Having them suggests that you're working through anxiety and revealing the phobias that govern so much of our activities."

View your next dream not only as a necessary biological process, but as a window to your soul. You might find creative inspiration for a best-selling novel or better understand your work-related angst. Perhaps you'll reduce stress that could lead to illness. There are plenty of choices for dream exploration today, including online discussion groups, workshops, books, Internet sites, and alternative healing therapists to help you more vividly recall your dreams and the emotions and insights they symbolize.

Never Settle

There are those who believe an academic credential, job title, or salary level will bring them satisfaction at work. And there are others who let their instincts and heart lead them to make a career change. The opportunity for change is yours and is in your control. Remind yourself that you have a lot to offer. Take all of your wonderful traits and find the right person, job, or path to appreciate them. Your skills and talents are portable. The real loss is when you do not value your assets. Changing your direction gives your personal and work life a different feeling.

Too many people tolerate disappointing jobs for years, even decades. Laziness and complacency are common culprits. For others, it's the judgmental opinions of family and peers that stall them from making a move.

Living the Dream

Bernard Spigner, host, *The Midday Show with Bernard Spigner*, WCTC 1450 AM, Central New Jersey Talk Radio

Look around your office. Chances are, while a handful of your colleagues truly delight in their work, many more of them simply show up and go through the motions. If you find yourself clock-watching for much of the workday, it's time to question why you took your job in the first place. Was it a pitstop you made because it was convenient and uncomplicated? Did it seem like a reliable source of income? Here's what Bernard Spigner had to say:

"I always wanted to be in broadcasting. Instead, after college graduation, I took a 'secure job,' driving an auto parts delivery truck to pay off my school loans. I kept a toe in broadcasting by volunteering to be the assistant producer of New Jersey Nets games. Two years later I decided I needed a 'suit and tie career.' I was on the fast track and moving up the ladder every six months or so . . . until the company was bought by another . . . and I was back to driving a truck. I decided that, if I wanted to be a broadcaster, I just had to do it. I showed up at Shadow Traffic's headquarters one day. They needed an assistant editor; however, the starting salary was only $11,500! Then I came up with an idea. I would drive a truck three days a week and work at Shadow the other two. I eventually rose to be general manager of Shadow. If you make a lot of money but are not happy with your profession, you are really only satisfied every other Friday . . . that being payday. I'm happy every day working at a job I love."

Would you stick things out in an unhappy marriage? How about a losing financial investment? What are the potential risks and rewards from owning up to a career mistake? After all, work shouldn't be just an income generator, but a source of pride and pleasure.

No matter what stage of life you're at, reevaluate your motivation level at work. If it doesn't hit seven on a scale of one to ten, it's probably time to cut your losses and switch gears. At the end of the day, it's your happiness you're shortchanging.

Gonna Make You a Star

Do you have the "it" factor? Meredith Fox knows star quality when she sees it. As executive producer for the hit TV talent show *Star Search*, she and her colleagues auditioned 10,000 pop star hopefuls for just fourteen contestant spots on the program. "For better or worse, the whole idea that someone can be plucked from obscurity and made a famous star is very appealing," she said. The winner of *Star Search* lands $100,000 and a recording contract with a major music label. But doors are not just opened for the winner. All the finalists get valuable exposure and get a jump-start to their careers as well.

"Many get agents and managers as a result of the exposure they receive. They perform in music videos and open for big-ticket concert acts," Fox explained. "You absolutely have to have both raw talent and the desire to pursue your passion, because even if you win, there's no guarantee you'll have a long, successful career," she said.

Persistence has also helped many candidates get ahead. "There were people who had unsuccessful auditions last year, but they kept working and practicing each week and we put them on this year. You have to always work to improve what you're doing," Fox added. "Just standing up in front of a room of judges is a great act of bravery. You have just over one minute to sing or dance your heart out. While we try to make the experience as positive as possible, at the end of the day it's still a competition. You have to get out there and want to win," said Fox.

Sacrifices, fear of competition, and pressure behind the scenes often cause many people to give up on their creative talents and rethink their caviar dreams. Lack of preparation—whether literally or emotionally—is the most common reason people blow their shot at the big time. Ask yourself if you are truly psychologically ready to put yourself out there for your talent or dream. Do you spend a certain amount of time each week working on your art or networking for a better job? Or do you flop out in front of the television. Do you put aside money every month into a nest egg for starting your own business—even if it means getting a second job? Many people sabotage their dreams because they're afraid of failure. However, just as often, people are afraid of making it big! Are you afraid that your family, friends, or spouse will be threatened by your success? Would becoming recognized in your field necessitate moving to another city? To get to the next level, you need to be yourself and have fun. Charisma and personality are the icing on the cake," said Fox.

The Power Behind the Throne

Maybe you've got good looks, sex appeal, and talent, but you freeze up in the spotlight. It happens to most people. Yet, if glitz and glamour are what you crave, you can still carve out a place for yourself in the entertainment and media worlds, even if you can't overcome your stage fright. In television and talk radio, for example, some of the greatest talent exists *behind* the limelight. Though you never see or hear the producers of today's hottest media programming, their efforts are often the wind beneath the wings of the celebrated on-air personalities they support.

Michelle Anton's life experience has well prepared her for her current role as executive producer of *Dr. Laura*, the nationally syndicated personal advice radio show. Originally from Brooklyn, New York, she was inspired by Oprah Winfrey as a teen. "I idolized her and wanted to do TV too. I wanted to give a voice to people who didn't have one," she said.

Michelle held jobs in fashion, advertising, and makeup sales before landing her first television gig in Los Angeles. As an assistant to a producer of *Soul Train,* she "learned that jobs have shelf lives. Wherever you're at, it may expire on its own."

While producing a TV pilot in Chicago, a lifelong dream became a reality. "I was hired as a freelance producer for *Oprah.* It's very fast paced and demanding. The only thing you can do is hit the ground running. You're not in it for the money or the glamour. You're in it because it's your calling," she said.

An admitted workaholic, Michelle soon burned out from wearing the hats of both producer and mom. "I needed a break and had to rethink my life's purpose," she admits.

Although she hadn't considered talk radio before, in 1991 a friend and producer of *Dr. Laura* suggested she work there, since the hours were more convenient.

"At that point, all I knew of Dr. Laura was that she was from Brooklyn and very opinionated. But I went into the job with fresh eyes and ears and we clicked right away," said Michelle. In her three and a half years with the live call-in show, Michelle has risen to the unique challenges of reality programming. "Every single day you start fresh. You don't know what's going to happen. But I've found a career that allows me to help and empower people," she said.

Michelle puts her success down to a variety of factors, the most important of which is to network hard. "I always had the impression that if you did a good job, it was enough, but I found out that there is a lot to be said about *who you know.* It's about the relationship."

She's also a believer in powering up every morning: "I often begin my day with a 5:30 A.M. conference call with two other professional women. We set goals and hold each other accountable for different things we want to achieve in our professional life."

Preparation is key. "Before each show, I surf the Web and scan roughly twenty newspapers for articles of interest to our audience. With roughly 12 million listeners and 20,000 attempted calls per hour, I screen each of the thirty people Dr. Laura talks to throughout the program."

Celebrity has its obvious perks, but it's not for the thin-skinned. Along with your art or talent, very often your personal life is considered fair game for examination and critique. What is most alluring to you about having a high-profile status? Is it the attention? Money? Power? You can attain all three without ever risking your self-esteem or privacy. Think of all the cinematic geniuses behind our biggest box-office hits or the producers who create today's hottest pop music songs. Fame for its own sake is a shallow goal. Instead, aspire to doing quality work that you enjoy. Don't worry, if you are truly talented, you'll get your fifteen minutes at some point.

Wearing All the Hats

If you dream about running your own business, consider this: Are you ready to be your company's public face? Prepared to think about your work all day, every day? Willing to do the work of two or three people when your employees have called in sick? Do you know what it's like to be solely responsible for something?

Many people compare business to war because you really do become your own general when you make the decision to create your own business entity. But the good news is that when you give in to your instinctual, entrepreneurial drive, your potential opportunities increase.

"Every day is a free spin on the roulette wheel," agreed Joe Casale, the owner of Aqua-Mechanics, Inc., a swimming pool repair company located in Long Island, New York. "If you just accept a job for short-term security, it takes you out of the game. You lessen your chance of creating your own windfall," he said.

As a young, newly married man in his twenties, Joe jobhopped from electronics to construction in search of a financially and mentally satisfying occupation. "My uncle could have got me different union jobs, with great benefits, but I felt that if I took one of them,

I'd never go into my own business, something I'd longed to do since I was a kid. It was a scary time because I needed money and was living hand to mouth," he recalled.

Living the Dream

Robin Segal, owner, Massage Massage

For nearly a decade, Robin Segal worked as a policy analyst for the U.S. Department of Energy. Routinely stressed out, Segal's one self-indulgence was to treat herself to a massage. Unfulfilled in her work, she used her knack for research to investigate the massage-therapy field and uncovered a niche for corporate massage. In 1998, she founded Massage Massage, an on-site chair massage service, which targets Manhattan workplaces. To legitimately practice there, Segal completed training at the Swedish Institute, received her license in massage therapy, and began to network herself in New York's prominent professional and trade organizations. After years of a steady income, Segal was able to self-fund her venture and cover start-up costs, including massage chairs, small advertisements, and a Web site. Today, Massage Massage boasts a network of thirty licensed and insured massage practitioners who are contracted out for different jobs.

Besides her seven-day workweeks and having to use her home phone as a business line, the greatest challenge in Segal's line of work is that her reputation must sparkle. But so far, the rewards of entrepreneurship seem to outweigh the demanding effort. "We're literally giving employees a pat on the back. I'm enjoying every minute of it."

Unwilling to lead a second-rate existence, Joe struck out on his own and created a company, now in its thirtieth year. "I didn't want to throw away years. Instead, I chose a life of excitement. I didn't always know how much money I'd take home week to week, but I was confident I'd make it."

Not everyone is cut out to run his or her own show. When the accounts payable start piling up, the competition closes in, or you've got an irate customer, the buck stops with you. But you are the choices you make. If you don't give entrepreneurship a shot, you've only got your insecurity to blame for letting your dream slip away. If you stick to your vision and take pleasure in your work, your "success" will be the natural joy you receive from doing what you love to do.

A Second Shot

Perhaps you've already built a thriving company. Now what? You may easily be able to afford to do whatever you want, including nothing. But like many type-A entrepreneurs, you may feel that retiring to a Caribbean island is simply not an option you want to pursue. It's likely that you are too much of an achiever, and the sudden loss of identity could be emotionally paralyzing. It's time to find a new dream to pursue.

There are plenty of ways to remain productive and keep your battery running. Some self-made success stories choose to sell their business, but still remain aboard as a big-shot executive. Some take off for months at a time, exploring the earth's natural wonders in search of spiritual enrichment. Others choose the philanthropic route, creating charities or taking up fundraising causes.

For intellectual stimulation or to stay competitive, you may wish to return to school. To expand or redirect their business initiatives, many seasoned executives are enrolling in Executive MBA (EMBA) programs. Take Dick Raymond, president and founder of Terra Systems, a Delaware-based environmental consulting and contract firm. Throughout the years he spent building his business, he had been narrowly focused on its technical aspects. "I had lost touch with the economic realities," he said.

Living the Dream

Dan Storper, CEO, Putamayo World Music

As a young boy, Dan Storper was fascinated by world travel and culture.

After earning a college degree in Latin American studies, he traveled through South America, where he visited a funky coastal town in the Putamayo River Valley. The stunning beauty of the region sparked the idea for a business venture. In 1975, Dan opened the first of seven apparel and handicraft stores in New York City. He designed his own ethnic-inspired contemporary clothing line, which was a hit with neighborhood residents and celebrity clientele alike. To further enhance his patrons' shopping experience, Dan began playing authentic world music in his stores. The music struck such a chord with customers that Dan knew he was on to something. Since 1993, Dan's Putamayo World Music label has produced over 100 CDs chronicling music from around the globe. The company has sold more than 10 million albums, including a series for kids. With no intention of retiring, Dan enjoys the fruits of his success. "The most rewarding thing is to get an e-mail from someone who bought a music compilation and then took the trip of a lifetime to the country it came from."

To sharpen his financial wit, Raymond enrolled in the EMBA program at Temple University's Fox School of Business and Management. The degree is aimed at upper- to midlevel managers from all industries. It takes about twenty-two months to complete the degree, and courses are offered on alternating weekends. "The biggest challenge for me was time management," said Mr. Raymond. "After the first semester, I was spending thirty or more hours a week studying and working on projects, in addition to operating my business full-time," he explained. Fortunately, Raymond's employees were supportive and, overall, he said it was an enjoyable experience.

So far, the benefits have outweighed Raymond's laborious commitment. "We're competing in a $2 billion industry," he said. "Without the MBA, I think people in my position are at a disadvantage. It's very competitive and small companies have to be two steps ahead of the big guys. Now, it's much easier for me to put myself in my clients' shoes, talk their language, and understand what their needs are. We've acquired a small firm since I completed the program and have launched a couple of new avenues. Without the degree, the execution would have taken longer," he said.

You Can't Take It with You

Think back to your childhood. What were your dreams? If you hate your job, what do you wish you could be doing? It's never too late to find a new passion. Now is a great time to go back to school and pursue a degree or an abandoned dream.

If one door closes, another will open, but you have to keep knocking. In your forties, society may be less forgiving, but you still have a body of experience. Have the courage to jump into an area that you were afraid to before. Discover your wisdom. Seasoned citizens have an advantage over those in their twenties and thirties. They have more humor and understanding and realize that losses can leave you with more perspective and gratitude for the full range of life's experiences. Whatever age you are, it's time to do the following two things:

1. *Identify your interests.* Who else shares these interests? What clubs or organizations focus on this and can you join them?
2. *Think about how you would like your eulogy to read.* Do you want to be remembered for your income level? The sports car you drive? How about the executive job title you held?

Truly creative people get bored with monetary success alone. They have an incessant need to reinvent themselves, their companies, and the directions they take. Such creative types also tend to be emotional and sensitive. They empathize with social problems. Some of businesses' biggest ideas have actually been inspired by injustice, poverty, misfortune, and educational initiatives.

Take stock of your real wealth—your happiness, fulfillment, and contentment—and if it doesn't add up to much, decide what would need to change and what would need to be done to make you emotionally and spiritually rich. Live your dream!

Summary

Reward rarely comes without endeavor, and endeavor comes with its own set of risks and decisions. Wherever you are in your life right now, you deserve to give yourself the chance to live the life that exists within your hopes and dreams.

Tips to remember:

- Never give up on your ambitions, even if you have been keeping them under a bushel for some time. It's never too late.
- Listen to your inner voice—even your actual dreams can tell you something about yourself and your goals in life.
- Don't settle for second best. Give it your best shot.
- Examine your potential and what following your dream will entail for you.

Chapter 2

Just Do It:
Don't Live a Life Unfulfilled

Often, it takes a dramatic wake-up call to make us aware of the good—and bad—things in our lives. Cancer survivors often talk of a new kind of momentum to their lives, one where they live in the moment, cherish what's good about their situation, and no longer put up with things that aren't. Personal tragedies have a strange way of striking up or reaffirming our desire to live our lives in the most authentic, committed way.

However, it shouldn't take a negative event to create this kind of awareness. You don't have to put up with a toxic work environment, an unfulfilling job, or lowly tasks indefinitely in the hope of garnering a promotion somewhere down the line. Instead, you need to have a goal mapped out and a route that you are actively following. If you really hate what you are doing, make the decision to bring about change. There's no time like the present. Consider the following:

- Do you come home from work in a bad mood?
- Do you get angry easily?
- Do you drink or eat to excess to try and bury your work life?
- Do you lack energy, focus, and drive?

By putting off life changes and stifling your true passion, you will not only be unhappy, but you may even make yourself mentally and physically ill.

In order to help preserve your health—and your mental well-being—until a better work situation comes along, seek out ways to make your everyday life more satisfying. A bad work situation can bleed into other areas of your life, sometimes before you're even aware of it. If you find it next to impossible to rise out of bed in the morning or are under- or overeating, you could be on the brink of depression and in need of professional help.

It's no coincidence that so many creative geniuses have been prone to bipolar disorder or manic depression—F. Scott Fitzgerald, Emily Dickinson, and Georgia O'Keeffe, just to name a few. When you are not free to express yourself or reach your highest potential, it can be demoralizing and even lead to mental illness, contends Dr. Richard O'Connor, a practicing psychotherapist from Canaan, Connecticut. "It's a fact that clinical depression is on the rise nationwide. Twenty percent of Americans will experience a major depression in their life cycle," said Dr. O'Connor. "There's a clear connection between how the world treats us and our self-esteem. If artists aren't able to find a way to express themselves at work, they're liable to be bored, anxious, or depressed. They need to find the right kind of challenge. If it's not on the job, it needs to be found somewhere else in their lives."

Oftentimes, a bad work situation is particularly depressing when there seems to be no immediate hope of getting out of it. Realistically, you may not be able to hand in your letter of resignation tomorrow; however, the most important thing is to focus on the steps you *can* take to make your dream a reality. If you're an artist, sign up for an art class or offer to teach one. Dreaming of starting your own business? Make an appointment with a banker to talk about small business financing. The point is to keep your dream moving forward even if your present situation feels more like quicksand than a paved road.

Living the Dream

Beverley Murphy, workaholic turned owner,
Be Yoga Studios of Florida and New York

"Until age twenty-five, I worked in New York's advertising industry. Back then, I was a yuppie type-A personality who tried every fitness fad du jour to stay fit and keep up with my life's treadmill pace. While vacationing in California, I stumbled into a beginner's yoga class and thought, *Wow, this feels really good.* Something clicked. Yoga is about self-love and acceptance. It's such a different mentality than trying to achieve some ideal that's not real.

"With my new outlook on wellness, I left the 'rat race' and shifted my career focus to alternative health. I earned a master's degree in health sciences and set out to become a professor. While pursuing my postdoctorate degree, I enrolled in the teacher training school at Yoga Zone and later instructed there. Six months later, I was making more as a yoga teacher than new professors do at Columbia. I had been employed by Yoga Zone for five years when my husband Bob and I decided to invest in the company, which changed its name to Be Yoga. The experience has been life changing and transformative. Without yoga, I couldn't succeed at wearing the hats of both businesswoman and mom."

Life Means More Than Just a Paycheck

According to the U.S. Bureau of Labor Statistics, in 2003, the number of jobless Americans hit an annual average of 8,774,000, a steep climb up from 5,692,000 in 2000. With so many companies cleaning house, more workers are reexamining their net worth and facing the fact that anyone is disposable.

Acutely aware that life takes highly unexpected turns, millions of Americans are reevaluating their life choices and reconnecting with inner passions.

Perhaps you've chosen, out of fear, to stay put and play it safe, even if you've grown disenchanted and unhappy at work. You may feel that you must go above and beyond your job description just to keep it or to maintain the lifestyle you've grown accustomed to. Continuing to work at a treadmill pace can cause you to burn out, damaging your health, family, and overall quality of life. The sooner you learn to savor and appreciate each day, the faster you'll want to take action and break out of a substandard work situation. Your life is too important to waste in a job you despise. There are inherent risks in moving in any direction in life. But if you follow your heart, you'll probably sleep better, live longer, and be more content. It's time to reassess your spiritual depth and move in a direction that lets your natural talents flourish.

Moving on Up

Is your problem one of constant clock-watching? Sharpening pencils? Perhaps you already have an artistic career or work for a creative company, but your job description does not include the kind of liberal thinking you wish you were putting to paper or the kind of music you would prefer to play. Before you cut loose from your employer (and steady paycheck), consider how you can expand or augment your current responsibilities in more creative ways.

If the hat you wear at work truly doesn't fit, don't throw in the towel. Explore other company divisions. If the grass seems greener in someone else's job title, find out what skills and credentials are required to earn that position. Think about where you would like to be in your organization and see if you can build a bridge to get there. Get the training needed to make that kind of switch. By mastering a new skill that can take you to another level within your job, you not only start to make new contacts, but you can also mobilize yourself to look for another position.

If it's a question of your free-spirited energy being drained, try rekindling your creative side:

1. Scan the magazine racks. Browsing media can give you great ideas or nuggets for research and may rekindle passions that lay dormant within you.
2. Take up a new or long-forgotten hobby. This should be something you can master for a sense of accomplishment (guitar, community theater, your family's genealogy, skiing).
3. Get back in touch with yourself. Spend time with animals or children (think zoos or youth centers). Their innocence and carefree nature can help to bring out your curious, fun-loving inner child.
4. Travel, go to museums, take a hike. Rediscover the wonder and beauty of nature. You will be awe-inspired and reinvigorated.
5. Team up with another creative mind. Bounce your ideas off of someone whose talent you admire and opinion you value.
6. Attend trade shows or conferences. At industry-specific events, you'll build up contacts, witness how other folks have turned their visions into reality, and feel that much closer to cashing in on your dreams.

Remember, though, that with great dreams, some sacrifice may have to be made. Would you take a pay cut to start at the bottom of your ideal career field? How about moving back home to save up money for night school? Gather inspiration from everything around you, but realize that you'll have to make tangible commitments of time, money, and hard work. It's called sweat equity!

One Step Back, but Two Steps Forward

Where there's a strong enough will, there's a way to escape a passionless life. Even the mightiest of armies understand that, to succeed on the battlefield, a platoon may need to retreat in order to strengthen its position. Can you relate to this tactic? Perhaps you are psyched up to open the café of your dreams, but are cash poor. Or, you're seeking a more creatively challenging occupation, but lack the education and training required to open doors for yourself.

Living the Dream

Tina Wilson, art director, Hallmark, Inc.

With a college degree in interior architecture, Tina started out in a creative-business role at Hallmark, designing and planning the decor for their stores. But she found the work too "rigid" and quickly became bored. Tina recognized the power of her employer's brand (Hallmark's share of the greeting card market is greater than 50 percent) and how fortunate she was to work for a company that fostered talent and creativity. So, she investigated other opportunities from within and became a photostylist. After five years with the firm, Tina now spends her days dreaming up concepts for cards and producing photo shoots and images that eventually end up in the racks of stores across the country—and in people's mailboxes. Tina says when she learns that one of her photo cards has hit the heart of what someone needed to express, "there's nothing like it."

In order to conquer the enemies that stand in your way (destitution, stiff competition, inadequate credentials) you may have to compromise or downsize your lifestyle today for a greener tomorrow. Keep the bigger picture in mind, and don't allow your ego to hold you back from fashioning a more self-directed and purposeful identity.

It can be hard to take a step back—be it in income, job title, or lifestyle—when you make a life change. Often the voice of fear can take hold and undermine your best efforts. If pursuing your dream necessitates going back to an entry-level job or living with your family, be appreciative of any support that is offered. Don't remind coworkers (or bosses) how overqualified you are for the position. Be grateful for the opportunity—even if it is paying you $20,000 less than your last position. If you have to live with your family, don't freeload! Establish a written or verbal agreement in regards to rent, household responsibilities, and overnight guests. Also, set a timetable for your "transition" job or living situation. Having a firm length of stay will make you more focused on your goal and stop depression from setting in if you find taking a step backwards becomes tough on your ego.

Keeping Your Vision Intact

Remember, there's no free ride to a more enriched life. Realizing your creative fantasy may cost you energy, stress, savings, and even personal relationships. You're likely to receive criticism and doubt—even from those who you may think have your best interests at heart. But if you allow fear and insecurity to bury your creative energy, you're the only one to blame for your disgruntled existence. You'll need to know how to handle some of the negative forces that you are sure to encounter as you aim for the stars.

Be wary of those who knock your ideas and goals. They may be threatened by or jealous of your creative knack. Guard and nurture your talents—they are your most powerful assets. When people try to make you look their way, continue to look your own way. Here are some tips for how to keep yourself on the path you've chosen:

- *Surround yourself with positive people.* The company you keep should be cheerful, supportive, and motivating.
- *Honor your parents, but when it comes to designing your future, think for yourself.* If mom and dad relentlessly shoot down your dream, let them say their piece, consider their feelings, but respectfully decline to follow them. It's *your* life.

Living the Dream

Beth Shevel, insurance agent turned veterinarian

For Beth, a love of animals and the desire to protect them began in childhood. Unfortunately, everyone, from guidance counselors to friends and family, slighted her aspirations of becoming a veterinarian. "Discouraged, I majored in English because it came easy," Beth said. "After college, I worked at an insurance firm to pay the rent. Almost a decade later, even after achieving management status, I was still unfulfilled." Then, her employer was bought out and Beth's retirement plan shot up to a sizable chunk of change. Wasting no time, she withdrew some of the money and reinvested in herself. "I viewed this as an opportunity to reexamine my career, go back to school, and pursue veterinary medicine. I moved into the basement of my parents' home so I could save money and attend school." Now in her last year of vet school at The University of Iowa, thirty-something Beth owes $70,000 in student loan debt. But she is more poised and pumped up than ever before to jump-start her new career. "I'm surprised at what you can deal with if there's enough passion behind it," she exclaimed proudly.

- *Keep your job hunt or pet project under wraps at the office.* Coworkers may resent your drive and attempt to sabotage your plan. Bosses could also take a dim view of your pursuing other professional/creative interests.
- *Stick to your own vision.* If you've always been one who sees things others' don't, realize that part of excelling at your art is learning not to conform.
- *Determine whether or not your current work environment is poisoning your creative process.* Do your colleagues spend their mornings surfing out great travel deals on the

Internet or catching up with e-buddies? If your coworkers don't share your enthusiasm and drive, you may need to switch teams or think about becoming your own leader.

- *Put yourself in a place where new ideas are encouraged.* It may be that your values are at odds with those of your employer. If your boss is closed-minded, let your original thinking breathe in a more approachable atmosphere.
- *Don't get caught up in gossiping and office politics.* Don't engage in such energy-zapping activity. If others are gossiping about you, use damage control and confront the culprit(s) one on one. If power struggles take precedence over business objectives, it could be time to remove yourself from such depleting forces.

Though you may feel imprisoned in your current occupation, you are not literally chained to your office cubicle. You have a choice to painfully grin and bear it or to use your experience to create a more meaningful, rewarding existence. If self-employment seems totally beyond reach, take comfort in knowing that droves of frustrated hired hands have successfully gone solo within the past decade. According to the U.S. Bureau of Labor Statistics, there were 10.3 million self-employed persons in the United States in 2003, up from 9.9 million in 2002.

Hardly surprising, since anybody who claims a paycheck has a tale of what it's like to endure office politics, have an idea backburnered, or a promotion request rejected.

No More Excuses, No More Delays

Why wait until the clock strikes 12:01 A.M. on New Year's Day to examine your happiness? Determine those areas in need of improvement and go after them with a realistic action list. Ask yourself if you are banking on fate to change your career status. Faith alone is unlikely to land you the work of your dreams. While some may need to kick a self-defeating habit, others may seek a more urgent, all-or-nothing approach to revamping their work life. Decide which category you fall into and make tomorrow the day you start taking control of your future.

Living the Dream

Jeffrey Yamaguchi, jobhopper
turned self-published author

After eight frustrating years in the real world, this young writer has cultivated a loyal following among those in need of comedic relief from their daily grind. At age twenty-eight, Jeffrey edited *Working for the Man: Stories from Behind the Cubicle Wall, Vol. 1* (Stroboscope Productions), a compilation of writings about the ulterior natures of coworkers, ways of avoiding work, horrible bosses, and the everyday humiliation that many job hunters face. Instead of shopping his book idea to the majors, Yamaguchi opted to self-publish it. Today, the witty, knee-slapping page-turner can be purchased at independent book shops, a few major online booksellers, and at the author's own Web site, which receives 10,000 hits a week and encompasses a growing online community. Jeffrey is currently developing programs for an online publisher and community for authors. He now views his career as project oriented and is already working on his second book.

There will always be reasons why you shouldn't, or couldn't, pursue a life you're more passionate about. Have the courage to take risks. Instead of wondering what might have been, try a bit of soul searching and crush the obstacles that may be preventing your creative juices from flowing. Power yourself up with positive thinking and avoid using clichéd rationalizations for rejecting your true calling.

The following are just some of the worries, concerns, and excuses that may be holding you back:

Excuse #1: "I'm too old"

Regardless of your age or career stage, isn't life too short to waste a single day in a job title that doesn't suit you? Folks in their fifties and sixties are increasingly proving that their acquired knowledge, experience, and staying power are traits they can transfer to second careers and new business opportunities. Don't put off a career change just because you'll be thirty or forty or fifty or whatever seems to be the age of no return. Remember, you're going to be thirty (or forty or fifty) anyway. Is it better to be that age and (still) be unfulfilled?

Excuse #2: "I have a lot of emotional baggage weighing me down"

Like a computer with too much garbage loaded on its hard drive, when you have unfinished business (a broken heart, family feuds) bothering you, such distractions can eat up your energy and hold you back. Discover what keeps your battery running and find a way to keep it charged up. If you're hung up on a difficult relationship dilemma, give yourself breathing room and walk away from it for a while. Or take a short trip to recharge. Often, solutions come to us when we distance ourselves from a problem.

Excuse #3: "The road to my goal just seems like too long a haul"

The pursuit of happiness is often a lengthy, trying process. But with enough motivation behind you, you can achieve more gratification in your work. You may need to take a step back in order to move forward. Realize that passion doesn't come cheap and there's no magic pill to swallow for instant results. It takes strategy, skill, and resolve to formulate a business idea and turn it into a money-making venture.

Excuse #4: "I'm worried about where the money will come from"

Ask any accomplished artist—there's no free ride to success. But honestly, can you put a price tag on the ability to express yourself at work and overcome the Sunday night back-to-work-tomorrow slump? You may need to take a pay cut, downsize your lifestyle, or moonlight for extra money, but where there's a will, there's a way to bankroll your dream.

Excuse #5: "My significant other/family/friend won't support my decision"

How do your intimate relationships grow and flourish? Consider going to therapy to discuss your ideas in front of an unbiased third party. If your partner or family member continues to discourage your creative ambition, despite encouragement from others around you, perhaps you need to make some hard decisions about your relationship with that individual. At the very least, you may need to minimize the input they have in your new career/ life direction.

Excuse #6: "I'm concerned about my kids"

Sure, children require life's basic necessities. But you can provide these for them and more—moral guidance, discipline, love—while still tending to your own wants and desires. Besides, if you don't shoot for the stars, what kind of example are you setting anyway?

Excuse #7: "I just don't have the energy"

Too often we cast aside our inherent desire to relax and replenish in order to satisfy our spouse, boss, parent, or child. But living such a selfless existence can be a slippery slope. Aside from the ramifications to your physical and mental health, you risk endangering your employment status and financial health, too.

Living the Dream

Lee Risler, owner, Kiwi Sandals

California shoemaker Lee Risler has created a successful business of handcrafting fine leather footwear. But his life has been anything but an easy stroll. In March of 2000, Lee's van was side-swiped by another motorist, causing it to tumble off the road into a woodsy ravine fifty feet below. For three days he was trapped in his vehicle—his left arm pinned between the roof and heavy tree limbs. Desperate to free himself, he amputated his own arm with a pocketknife. Rescue workers extricated Lee and rushed him to the hospital. Though doctors couldn't save his arm, Lee's spirit remained unscathed. With the help of his family, Lee was exhibiting at craft shows again, only six weeks after the car wreck. Wearing a prosthetic arm he designed himself, Lee and his family work full-time, producing upwards of eighty pairs of sandals every week. Today, his Kiwi sandals sell like hotcakes at upscale craft fairs throughout the United States, and he grosses around $60,000 annually. Grateful to be alive, Lee is happy to still be doing the work he so enjoys. "No matter what happens to you, you can keep going," he said. "If you go long enough, success will come from your effort."

Excuse #8: "I don't have any business experience"

Don't get discouraged if you majored in art history and not economics. Every successful businessperson had to take his or her "first steps" and make plenty of mistakes before achieving gold and glory. Rid yourself of self-doubt and, instead, concentrate on what drives you. For an overview on how to start a company from A to Z, you can always take a course in skills for small business owners. Research class instruction options online, through community colleges, and continuing education programs.

Remember one thing: Nothing is insurmountable. People have overcome incredible difficulties—physical, emotional and financial—to realize their dreams.

So what's holding *you* back? It takes energy to resist your sixth sense and true desires. Why not redirect that time and brainpower to search out a more befitting job or career? If you've been blessed with sound health and freedom, don't take this good fortune for granted. Instead of blaming other people and factors for your discontentment at work, chart your own course and live your life without regrets.

Making Lemons into Lemonade

Conversely, while you may be deliberating about changing jobs or redefining your career, look out—events may overtake you.

In today's corporate climate, workers can expect to face a layoff at least once in their career due to downsizing, mergers, and acquisitions. A young person today may have eight to ten jobs in their lifetime. After hearing "the news," your emotions may range from shock to denial. If you're pressured to sign a severance package then and there, simply refuse because you can't be objective at that moment. Losing your temper or acting hostile can work against you if you plan to obtain job references and maintain a good reputation in your industry. If you've been fired legitimately (job elimination, reorganization), your goals are more severance pay and other post-termination benefits. Severance pay is usually based on your tenure. Depending on your status, achievements, and the industry you're in, you may request anywhere from one week to a month for each year of employment. Year-end bonuses are often discretionary and based on performance, but if you were due one, argue that your firing deprived you of the right to receive it. If this fails, try to settle for half the amount.

With health benefits, try to extend the grace period of coverage a few months, especially if your plan covers your family. Employers often grant this request to make you feel you were treated respectfully. If securing an immediate income is crucial, offer to remain on board as a consultant, while making your transition to a new job.

Living the Dream

John Roblin, owner, 8thPlanet.com

A graphic designer from Long Island, New York, Roblin had been through several layoffs in his career, always due to corporate buy-outs. "After the last layoff, I decided to take control of my own destiny and start a business," Roblin said. "I networked with my contacts and used my cushion of severance pay to advertise and mail out brochures. The more I talked to potential clients, the more confident I became in my salesmanship. "Today, my phone doesn't stop ringing. Self-employed for over seven years, I don't miss the full-time job I left. Today, my graphic and Web site design studio provides more creative satisfaction then I ever imagined. I get positive feedback and recognition from clients and I really like that. Unaware of what the distant future may bring, I know one thing for sure. No one can buy this company out from me unless I want them to."

Outplacement assistance is a helpful benefit to secure as well. Such support helps you redirect your career goals, update your resume, and devise a marketing strategy for landing your next job.

Consider hiring a lawyer to ensure that you receive the best severance package possible. Since lawyers are emotionally detached, they can save you mental stress, too.

If you have any kind of redundancy money, you may now have

some of the capital necessary to make your dreams reality. If you become unemployed through no fault of your own, you may be entitled to benefits and retraining. Contact your state's unemployment insurance office for more information.

Living the Dream

Chris Albrecht, president of Original Programming, HBO

Since Chris Albrecht was promoted to his current position in 1995, the cable network has cranked out a strand of utterly addictive, award-winning comedy and drama series, including *Sex and the City* and *The Sopranos*. Throughout his industry, Chris is known for his self-initiating attitude and razor-sharp instincts for detecting a hit story line. Raised in Laurelton, New York, Albrecht attained a bachelor's degree in dramatic literature from Hofstra University. By age twenty-two, he co-owned The Improvisation, the famed Manhattan nightclub. He later went on to work for International Creative Management, signing such star talent as Jim Carrey and Billy Crystal. "As an agent, you need to make something happen every day or you haven't had a good day. You don't wait for things to come," he said. In 1985, Albrecht joined HBO as head of West Coast programming, a move many friends and colleagues frowned upon. Albrecht, however, credits his risk-taking style for much of his success. Reviewing roughly fifty scripts a week, his team bases its decision to "greenlight" a production based on a gut feeling—not a test audience.

At some point or another, we're all dealt a bad hand. Are you the type of person who learns from your setbacks, or do you allow misfortune to define you? When the tide turns against you, you have a choice—to be bitter and resentful, or to rise up and accept your circumstance as a test. Hidden inside each challenge, there's usually a lesson or buzzing opportunity just waiting to be brought to light.

Taking the Bull by the Horns

If you're one of the millions of people each year who has been laid off or forced to resign or retire prematurely, remember the old adage "Success is the best revenge." The end of one employment situation is just the beginning of another. For one thing, you can eliminate many of the sticking points against making your own way. You no longer have to worry about doing the right thing or being irresponsible for quitting your job. In Chinese, crisis and opportunity are the same word. The decision has been made for you—now make it happen! Above all, don't beat down your sense of self-worth after getting fired. Look upon the transition as a great blessing, not a disaster. Instead, consider your newfound freedom an opportunity.

Summary

Thinking long term can be tough, especially in this here-and-now society, but by looking at the horizon rather than at your feet, you will get a much better perspective of your life goals. It can also help you endure temporary hardships and even setbacks. Happiness and fulfillment are a lifelong journey.

Tips to remember:

- Finding an outlet for your talents can help you improve your mental and physical health, so don't let "the glums" stop you from setting out on the path to a better life. Try looking for a better slot within the company you currently work for. Your skills may be better used in a different capacity.
- Think about stripping things right back to basics—perhaps going back to school in some form is the right move. If so, figure out what downsizing your life will mean and what sacrifices you may have to make in the meantime.

- If you're at a crossroads thanks to outside influences, like being laid off, look on it as a blessing in disguise. Remember, in Chinese, the words for crisis and opportunity are the same. You now have the perfect reason to work toward your true goals.

Chapter 3

Artpreneurship Rising:
Join the Ranks of the Creative Class

Only a decade ago, the self-employed were perceived as a notch below those who worked in hot corporate jobs for *Fortune* 500 companies. Today, being entrepreneurial is not only sexy, but for many people it is the best way to earn a decent living. The good news is that there has never been a better time to learn and sell a skill, capitalize on your art or craft, and make your dream come true.

Creativity has actually become a highly prized commodity in our economy. Those who use it as part of their basic job description are part of a burgeoning new socioeconomic class, according to Richard Florida, professor of regional economic development for the Heinz School of Public Policy and Management at Carnegie Mellon University and author of *The Rise of the Creative Class . . . and how it's transforming work, leisure, community and everyday life* (Basic Books).

While being educated still has a strong correlation to economic success, Florida argues that "you don't need a formal education to be a member of the creative class, which now constitutes roughly 30 percent of our workforce. Just look at Bill Gates and Michael Dell—both dropped out of college."

So which industries are driving the creative economy? Core employers include research and development, TV and radio, publishing, toy and game companies, and software.

While creative class members earn twice as much as those in the working class (those in production, operations, transportation, repair, maintenance, and construction work), they are not motivated solely by money. According to Florida, "They want challenge, responsibility, flexibility, and an ability to express themselves at work. They want an idiosyncratic job contract—not one size fits all."

If you're ready to join this elite professional club, there are a few signature characteristics Florida claims you should possess:

1. You must highly regard meritocracy. In other words, you believe that people can and should get ahead on merit and skills. You're ambitious and want to move up based on ability and effort.

2. Since the nature of creative work is cyclical, you should not be afraid to work long but flexible hours (forty-nine or more a week).

3. You take your identity from the kind of work you do, not from the company or client you work for.

4. You're willing to trade job security for autonomy, and conformity for the freedom to move from job to job and to pursue interesting projects and activities.

5. You spend a lot of time marketing yourself to prospective employers and thus view your physical appearance as a means for creative expression. You believe you are more marketable if you look your best.

6. You require more than financial compensation to make yourself happy and stay committed to your work. Beyond the paycheck, you need to know that your work has an impact and that your position offers you the chance to learn and grow.

If this all sounds like you, you are either in the creative class or on your way there.

Creative Centers

For proof that the creative class is shaping how we live, work, and do business, look no further than today's most creative cities. It's no coincidence that real-estate prices in these creative centers increase 10 to 20 percent each year and rank highly as centers of innovation, human capital, and employment growth, according to Florida's research.

Creative climates also commonly share what Florida calls "The Three T's"—technology, talent, and tolerance. These creative centers tend to cater to multiple industries and diverse minority groups, immigrants, and alternative lifestyles. Residents seek to take responsibility for change in their communities, are politically and socially active, and lobby to dismantle barriers to creativity, such as intolerance, poverty, bad schools, exclusivity, and social and environmental degradation.

America's Top Ten Creative Cities, according to the December 2003 edition of Florida's book are:

1. Austin, TX
2. San Francisco, CA
3. Seattle, WA
4. Boston, MA
5. Raleigh-Durham, NC
6. Portland, OR
7. Minneapolis, MN
8. Baltimore, MD
9. Sacramento, CA
10. Denver, CO

Are you ready to relocate to more artistically stimulating surroundings? Before you uproot yourself and your family, you'll need to contemplate the pros and cons. Will this move accommodate both you and your partner's needs? What is the cost of living in your new zip code? Will your income potential be affected by relocating?

If so, will you be comfortable adjusting? Estimate how long it will take for you to find new work or get your business going. Do you have a financial cushion to fall back on while you're unemployed? If your family isn't supportive of your move, whom will you turn to for emotional support?

Living the Dream

Monica Ramirez, founder, Zalia International, Ltd.

Monica Ramirez is a thirty-year-old Latina beauty who wouldn't ever be caught looking unpolished. "My mother worked as a rep for Mary Kaye Cosmetics for many years," said Monica. Inspired by her mom, as a young girl Monica grew passionate about the beauty industry and discovered that finding the right makeup was a constant challenge. "I always had an issue with the tone and coloring. It mismatched the rest of me," said Monica. With Hispanic women in mind, Monica tirelessly investigated the Hispanic beauty industry to determine what competition existed and talked with other Latina women to explore their cosmetic needs. Her research convinced her that she had struck a business niche and that the target market was huge. "Cosmetics are a $15 billion industry in the United States and, by 2010, the Latin population will be the largest minority group in the nation," she said. In December of 1999, Zalia International, Ltd. was born. Today, Zalia makeup products are sold and distributed through salons in New York, Florida, and Puerto Rico that cater to Hispanic women. The company also conducts makeup parties as fundraisers for community and nonprofit groups. Monica is now seeking additional funding to realize her goal of running a fully international business.

The New Color of Money

The complexion of America's small business climate is shifting, according to research by the Small Business Association. Today, women from every ethnic background, age bracket, and industry are embracing their entrepreneurial spirit and turning their passions into profits. Out of 22.9 million businesses in the United States today, 5.4 million are owned by women, which generates $819 billion in revenues and employs more than 7 million workers.

Minority entrepreneurs are also keenly aware of the role that race plays in business. From cosmetics to beauty salons, from filmmaking to real-estate development, they are creating companies to serve multicultural populations faster than anyone. As of 1997, 5.8 percent of all U.S. firms were owned by Hispanic Americans, 4.4 percent by Asian Americans, and 4 percent by African Americans, according to SBA research.

Are You a Closet Entrepreneur?

Though the distance and sacrifices vary from person to person, the rewards of going solo are often worth the climb. The first step toward self-employment is determining your readiness for this work style. The next is to determine what may be holding you back. Is it job security that worries you, or is it losing your steady paycheck?

Consider this: Companies downsize and restructure every day. Job security is a dying term affiliated with the "American dream" of yesteryear. Our modern-day fantasy includes a more personally fulfilling career, which affords us a balanced work and home life.

If you have a low tolerance for risk and dislike uncertainty, you're wise to cling to the corporate ladder. True entrepreneurs rid their minds of any self-doubt. They will take a step back to go forward, choosing to live cheaply today with an intense focus on a greener tomorrow. Whether they have scant start-up money or are fully backed by a venture capitalist, entrepreneurs are rich with ideas.

They concentrate on what drives them. Reaffirming your values will help you to zero in on the sort of occupation you need to create for yourself to best support your priorities. Once your light bulb has gone off, congratulate yourself. You'll know what your unique business vision is.

But hold on—a true taste of entrepreneurship won't come until you've entered the phases of market research, business planning, raising capital, marketing, promotion, and positioning for growth.

Understand that by choosing entrepreneurship, you are not choosing a new job, but rather an independent lifestyle. Your typical nine-to-five day will fade to memory. When you work for yourself, early on you will wear every hat. You'll take on the roles of bookkeeper, accountant, secretary, salesperson, and publicist—and all for no extra pay.

Though challenging, the rewards of self-employment are great. Instead of working at someone else's beck and call, your work is self-directed. You will no longer have to sacrifice your self-expression. In fact, your financial security will rely on it.

The Next Big Thing

It takes strategy to conjure up a business concept and turn it into a moneymaking venture. You need to know which trends are current and which are yesterday's news. If you're not a natural trend tracker, however, all is not lost. You can hire one.

Trend forecasting is a special service of some marketing-consulting firms. Typically, forecasters are brought on board to accumulate and analyze the personal habits and statistics about a client's customers, identify new business opportunities, and apply this insight to their clients' specific brands—hopefully way before the competition.

Techniques vary among future-based consultancies, but the fundamental skill that trend spotters possess is to stay connected to the world. Aside from reading everything they can get their hands on, such folks will typically monitor the top twenty television shows, first-run movies, best-seller books, and hit music in their effort to track trends in products, moods, and consumer behavior patterns. The more in touch they are with what's happening now, the more likely they are to identify emerging patterns.

Living the Dream

Helen Ficalora, hotel manager/jewelry designer

Jewelry is the most priceless of gifts, according to Helen Ficalora, who creates her own collections of pink, yellow, and white gold ring bands, earrings, necklaces, and pendants. While she enjoyed jewelry-making in high school, Helen became a full-time home-maker in Olympia, Washington. Nearly a decade ago, Ficalora resumed jewelry-making as a meditative hobby. "I go into a whole other realm. It's transformative," she explained. Her design technique involves hand carving, waxing, and casting original molds in the shape of flowers, angels, shells, and yoga poses, and all from a home studio. After test-marketing her products on friends, Ficalora expanded her side business to both mail-order and online catalogs. While trunk shows, advertising, and direct sales to select retail stores help to keep the orders rolling in, Ficalora is working with a business coach on a marketing plan to grow her company. But she admits she isn't sold on the idea of mass-producing her wares: "I don't know that I could continue the quality. Every item is made-to-order. Without this kind of personal attention and care, it wouldn't be as satisfying to me or to my customers."

Don't confuse a trend with a fad. Fads are more product oriented (pet rock, anyone?), while trends are about what motivates consumers to buy products. For example, specialty and exotic teas are growing in popularity. And Zagat's, the internationally renowned restaurant guide, has recently introduced a tea category to accommodate the rise of afternoon tea–tasting menus in elegant hotels and restaurants. This trend stems from a drift toward small indulgences. Stressed-out consumers have a growing need to indulge in inexpensive luxuries (spas, manicures, afternoon tea) to reward themselves. To try and predict the next big thing on the market, remain curious, be your own antenna, and think ahead of the curve. Luckily, ideas are all around you.

From Pastime to Profits

The one common denominator that all entrepreneurs have is tunnel vision. Often people don't think of such intense focus as a positive trait, but such perseverance will assure you victory. If you have repeatedly drawn blanks for a fruitful extra-income generator, focus on your natural gifts, hobbies, or personal mission.

Perhaps languages are your calling. If you're multilingual and able to teach such skills, career and business opportunities are boundless in the education field. Whether you teach language classes and seminars or author books on such subjects, professionals from a variety of industries need to know languages to enhance their resume, to attract new clients and customers, and to carry on daily contacts.

The climate is also ripe to take advantage of today's baby boom. For example, humdrum infant wear wasn't meeting the style expectations of those with fashionable tastes. Just take a clue from major retailers—The Gap, Old Navy, and Pottery Barn all now offer baby apparel and product lines. Offering everything from clothing to shoes and furniture, these new stores, products, and e-commerce sites are popping up by the dozen, targeting new parents and moms-to-be.

The maternity market is another hot target. One woman sells "baby masks"—papier-mâché kits women use to preserve the shape and size of their pregnant bellies. There are pregnancy masseuses and a wave of high-end maternity clothing lines springing up.

These days, any item that comes straight from the heart evokes a priceless appreciation. Consider selling your handmade garments, from dog coats and baby pullovers to home décor items.

Knitting is also making a big comeback. The industry serves a $300 to $500 million market. Upscale yarn boutiques are all the rage, selling top-quality yarns of distinct colors and textures and hosting trunk shows and knitting lessons. If you can teach others the trade, you may be able to pull in as much as $100 an hour for a private knitting lesson.

Living the Dream

Amy Sullivan, owner, Sully Saks

Several years ago, while riding the train home from her Manhattan day job, Amy Sullivan, then a thirty-two-year-old legal secretary from Long Beach, New York, spotted a teenage girl knitting a hat. "It was wintertime, and I decided that I wanted to learn how to do that," she explained. By the summer of 2002, Amy's hobby accidentally turned into a moneymaking opportunity. A devoted yoga student, Amy grew tired of lugging her yoga mat under her arm to class. So she found some yarn and crocheted her own bag to carry it in. "People started asking me where I got it. When I told them I made it, I was encouraged to sell them," Amy said. Today, Amy makes her bags at home and during her daily commute to and from work. The durable, stylish, all-cotton bags are available in an array of colorful solids and swirling patterns. Each Sully Sak costs $35 apiece. "I've never sold anything before. But now I'm actually starting a Web page on eBay so I can get the product out there," said the budding entrepreneur.

Sometimes you don't need to look that far to discover a source of personal pleasure and monetary gain. Are you a health and exercise nut? Do you subscribe to every home-beautifying/lifestyle magazine on the market? How often do you cook or bake for friends? Do you create your own holiday cards? Consider the ways in which you spend your free time. Our hobbies and leisure pursuits are great starting points for revenue streams.

Finding Your Niche

If you lie awake at night racking your brain for a fall-back plan or second-income generator, find a movement, trend, or something that works in a big way, and then drum up a way to tweak it for a specialized audience. The key to turning a unique idea, skill, or talent into a steady side gig is to pay attention in life—ideas are all around you.

For example, more women are looking for ways to get out of the house. Hosting book club, wine-tasting, jewelry, or lingerie parties are just a few fun activities with moneymaking potential.

Or how about teaching a new, high-tech, or specific skill? Almost everyone has a piece of knowledge that they can sell to someone else. Community continuing education centers are great outlets for you to market your expertise.

Here are some more ideas for where to look as you try to find the niche that suits you best:

Personal services—Can you save someone else time? Running errands for seniors, preparing someone's tax returns, or walking your neighbors' dogs are examples of valuable services to offer.

Gardening and landscaping—Consider the growing garden trade. Homeowners who lack the time or desire to plant and prune still recognize the importance of curb appeal today. Landscape design, maintenance, and retail gardening businesses are hot now. If you enjoy working in nice weather around nature, the field of horticulture covers a wide range of professional specialties. You can be an arborist, look after commercial greenhouses, and care for golf courses or large private estates. With a formal education, you'll learn about jet stream patterns and their effect on which plants grow best in certain regions.

Outdoors recreation work—For some folks, there is no separation between work and play. Such types are reluctant to punch a clock or limit themselves to an indoor office cubicle to earn their living. If you're a wilderness buff, perhaps you're ready to strike out on your own and take Mother Nature on as a business partner. Business ideas include kayaking/white-water rafting outfitter; guided mountain biking, photo trekking, backpacking, or rock climbing tour operator; or opportunities within the state park system.

Pet services—Could your business be going to the dogs? Upscale pet-related services and merchandise are bringing home the bacon—to the tune of $30 billion a year in the United States today according to a recent research study from Unity Marketing in Stevens, Pennsylvania. Pet foods, doggie daycare, shampoos, and even "pet pampering" spas and hotels are just a few of the products and services that make up the industry. If you have a knack for dog handling, dog obedience is another hot extra-income generator.

Workplace design—You could be a creator of the workplace of the future. As industries evolve, tomorrow's offices will entice us through hip, ergonomically correct furnishings, the use of color, and innovative lighting. The need for experts who can implement ergonomically correct conditions is rising. Areas of specialization include industrial workplaces, occupational safety, furniture design, computer hardware, human-computer interaction, product liability, consumer products, and virtual environments.

Feng shui consulting—Interest in feng shui has risen in recent years as more people seek greater levels of satisfaction and productivity in their career, business, and lifestyle. This ancient art promotes spiritual and material well-being by devising the best way to lay out your house or office. Certified experts are hired to do "readings" for both residential and commercial spaces. Consultants can charge between \$235 and \$1,000 for a two-hour consultation, depending on the size of a property. Some businesses will pay upwards of \$15,000 for large-scale projects. Field certification costs upwards of \$3,500 and includes class time, mentoring, and field training.

Living the Dream

Pamela Sheldon Johns, author of *The Healthy Gourmet Cookbook* (HarperCollins), *Parmigiano!* (Ten Speed Press), and *Italian Food Artisans* (Chronicle Books).

Passion is the main ingredient of success for this schoolteacher turned best-selling cookbook author.

"I began my career teaching cooking and food service to high school students with disabilities. On the side, I assisted at Ma Cuisine Cooking School, where many celebrity chefs guest lectured. Later, I worked for revered local chef/restaurateur Joachim Splichal. Though creatively challenging, the restaurant business wasn't my calling. In 1992, I landed my first book contract, opened my own cooking school, and began leading culinary workshops to Italy, which I still conduct today. I find writing about food essentially a sensual matter. The smell, the taste, the way it looks and feels, even the sound of it cooking, or when it's chewed. Much of successful communication is experiential. I think there's more satisfaction in speaking from the heart, instead of contriving something that might sell well."

Alternative health services—As our health-care system becomes more prevention-oriented, Americans are increasingly more accepting of alternative, holistic health, and wellness practices. Healing arts such as massage therapy, reflexology, acupuncture, and yoga are in demand by private and corporate clientele. Food items or eateries offering organic edibles free of processed ingredients, preservatives, and sugars are sought after by the health-conscious.

Grooming services—Thanks to the popularity of television shows such as *Queer Eye for the Straight Guy*, men are becoming more upfront about wanting to look and feel good about themselves. For these so-called metrosexuals, a new wave of relaxation havens specially designated for men are cropping up. Today's hottest services include facial bronzing, stone massage, organic facials, reflexology, and seaweed wraps.

Spiritual work—Spiritually minded people make humanity their life's work. Today there are plenty of creative job paths you can pursue if you feel inspiring others is your life mission. For example, religious craftspeople and artists (think of all the Judaica and Catholic supply shops, candleholders, jewelry charms, trinket boxes, decorative nativity art and collectibles); church camp counselor/director; religion writers and authors (even for religious greeting cards); and spiritual retreat leaders. These last folks lead trips to destinations with biblical/historical significance.

Senior-focused services—Don't forget the lucrative aging baby boomers. The fifty-five-plus population is an intelligent, active group. They need products, services, and information providers to meet their entertainment, education, and lifestyle needs. Today, there are senior-focused book authors, Web site developers, travel, insurance and real-estate companies, and computer training firms reaping profits from the older Americans they serve.

Business writing and services—If your skill is putting it in writing, hire yourself out as a business plan writer. Too many businesses lose out on new contracts, funding, or clients because they don't know how to communicate their message on paper. Businesses today have a need for marketing, strategy, lobbying, and proposal writing services. Also, the demand for freelance writers with specialties in grant writing, bio med, IT, economic development, and general business is high. Project work includes requests for proposals

(RFPs), corporate training guides, computer documentation, white papers, government licensing applications, legislative memos, and executive bios. Fees typically start at $100 per hour, or between $30,000 and $60,000 a year.

Home design and services—These days, home is where the art is. Thanks to baby boomers with discretionary income and a nationwide "cocooning" trend, interior decorating and design services are in demand. From guesthouses to second homes, vacation retreats to master bathrooms, those cashing in on the thriving home-fixings craze include architects, interior designers, landscape architects, and pool builders. Other jobs include project management professionals for furniture companies or corporate facilities and designers of hotels, healthcare institutions, retirement communities, and nursing homes.

Culinary services—By the same token, staying in is the new going out and people are entertaining in their homes more than ever. Dinner parties have made a big comeback. If you have culinary skills, you are in demand. Aside from catering, you may decide to give one-on-one cooking lessons, help prepare menus, or conduct demonstrations in your own home. For the many people trying to eat well, both for health and epicurean reasons, you can hire yourself out as a personal chef or nutritionist.

Keep Your Eye on the Prize

Do you boast the octave range of Whitney Houston? Or the grace of Baryshnikov on the dance floor? Without intense focus and determination, the world may never know or support your strong suits. Sometimes, the most gifted people quit. Perseverance is what separates successful artists from those who starve. If you don't go for it, you'll never get it.

Summary

Being an artisan, artist, or entrepreneur makes you a hot commodity, and the good news is you need the will, the talent, and the skill—not formal education. There are no barriers other than those that you set for yourself. So tear down your inner fear and set your skills free.

Living the Dream

Mindi Abair, recording artist

Mindi Abair is a hot new female saxophonist in a stereotypically male-dominated genre. Her debut smooth jazz album, "It Just Happens That Way" (GRP Records), has already sold 30,000 copies. To nurture her talent, Mindi accepted a scholarship at Boston's Berklee College of Music. Upon graduation, she trekked out to Los Angeles to pursue her artistic dreams. To support herself, she'd play her sax on the street, often earning $200 a day. "It's not exactly prideful, but it was better than saying, 'Do you want fries with that?' she said. One night, while performing at a small café, she got a major break. "John Tesh walked in and by the end of the night had asked if I wanted to tour with his band," she said. From there, Mindi toured with the Backstreet Boys and Mandy Moore, but she'd always return home to work on demo tapes and shop her material, hoping to break out as a solo artist. A Universal Music executive eventually recognized Mindi's unique image and sound. Today, Mindi is touring the country, performing for thousands of fans. "I've worked for this. Seeing people in the audience, knowing they came to see you play is a validation and so much fun," she said.

Tips to remember:

- Find your business niche. Look at other businesses, examine your skills, and see how they translate into the real world.
- No one is saying it's going to be easy. Your new direction will probably call for you to work long hours and invest plenty of sweat equity. But remember, it will pay off.

Chapter 4

The Real World:
It's Time to Put Your Business Hat On

So, you have the ingenuity and inventiveness it takes to drum up a business idea, but no prior experience. Sure, you'll have a lot of groundwork to do, but don't let a lack of experience in wheeling and dealing deflate your inspiration and drive.

Although it will take time to establish a client roster, from the get-go you can test out your idea on family, personal pals, and professional liaisons. Use their feedback to tweak your product, create a revenue model, define your target customer base, create a marketing mix, and craft an image for your company. This network of contacts will also prove invaluable for spreading initial word of mouth about your business.

To learn the ABCs of Business 101, consider taking a course or reading books on the subject. Free training programs and workshops are offered through the Service Corps of Retired Executives Web site *www.score.org*.

You don't need a Harvard Business School degree to give the American dream a whirl. Tenacity and enthusiasm go a long way when you're just starting out. There are countless stories of business tycoons who began their enterprises peddling their wares door to door or using their garages as manufacturing and distribution centers. Don't hesitate to reach out to successful businesspeople in your community. Passion is contagious. Whether it's sales leads, media exposure, technical assistance, or cold cash you need, speak up. You are your company's best spokesperson. Find someone in your local business community who can mentor you. You never know who may be willing and able to lend you support.

Living the Dream

Heather McCartney, president, Ethnic Edibles

Heather McCartney is president of Ethnic Edibles, a company that produces multicultural cookies and cookie cutters. "Inspiration for my company came when, after a memorable trip to South Africa, I replicated tribal masks as cookies. People didn't want to eat them, they looked so good!" she said. Though she personally financed the bulk of her endeavor, she secured a small loan through another nonprofit group that matches women entrepreneurs with funding. To gauge demand for her product, Heather distributed surveys among her friends, family, and coworkers and talked to Manhattan subway riders. She determined that her prime customers would be women, particularly mothers between the ages of thirty-two and fifty, as well as teachers, travelers, African Americans, and those who enjoy baking. Business took off in 1999 when, during Black History Month, Heather sent a press release to B. Smith, an acclaimed restaurateur and media figure. "She featured me on her TV show and in the premiere issue of her magazine. Today, I have a flourishing client list of stores, catalogs, and museum shops, including the Smithsonian Institute."

The Bottom Dollars

Hopefully, you've banked enough paychecks to be able to self-fund your creative venture. But supplies, advertising, and studio rentals don't come cheap. If you're strapped for the investment capital you need, it can feel like a Catch-22—you need to have money in order to borrow it. But if you require under $1,000 to start your creative endeavor, you can quickly raise the cash by taking on a short-term job. Consider the options that follow:

Direct sales

Today, there are over 11 million independent salespeople repping products such as Tupperware, lingerie, makeup, and home décor through in-home presentations or one-on-one selling. The practice involves the person-to-person sale of a product or service, away from a fixed retail location. Traditionally, direct sales have provided extra income for housewives, but hosting a sales party can be a great way to boost funds. It can also be a way to make contacts and cross market, if what you're selling is related to your fledgling business or talent. For example, if you're an aspiring chef or caterer, selling cookware can be a great way to network.

When scouting out potential opportunities, realize you may be required to participate in a training program. And since it's customary to earn your paycheck solely through commissions, the more referrals and appointments you get, the more you'll rake in.

Temping

Temping is also a great way to bring in some money while you develop your idea for a salable product or service. The benefits of this work style include making your own hours, avoiding office politics, and gaining exposure to different corporate environments or insight into the demands of a particular job and its growth potential.

As our economy grows more service based, today's contract workers comprise a wider spectrum of professions across the job board: administrative assistants, home health aides, computer engineers, marketing supervisors, and social workers are just a few of the occupations experiencing the largest growth rate.

Choosing this work means thinking of yourself as a commodity and being able to market and sell yourself. If you're uncomfortable with finding the work for yourself, your best bet is to work with a reputable agency.

Service jobs

Hotels and restaurants deploy hundreds of full-time and temporary workers seasonally and during holidays. Such personnel needs include waiters, banquet waiters, cooks (prep and line) carvers, on-site chefs, cashier and counter people, bus persons, dishwashers, bartenders, housekeepers, hosts and hostesses, and managers.

Retail can be a great way to earn cash around the holidays. Jewelers, chocolatiers, giftware companies, department stores, and florists top the list of businesses that typically beef up their workforces this time of year. Personnel are needed for customer service, sales, cashier, stock, greeting, and management functions. Such jobs can command between $8 and $11 an hour.

Security jobs are plentiful. If you're a high school graduate, can pass a drug test, and have no criminal record, you're eligible. Such work involves patrolling the corridors of shopping malls or the entrances to apartment buildings, offices, retail shops, or department stores.

It's a Matter of Money

Did you know that the vast majority of all businesses fail within five years? "In large part, this is due to undercapitalization," said Kris Solie-Johnson, president of the American Institute of Small Business (AISB). There are several steps you can take to make sure you don't fall at the first hurdle.

Generate early orders. Try to get customers to prepay for your product or services. With this cash-flow strategy, you'll have some initial funds to cover materials, machinery, and other start-up costs.

Apply for a microloan. Lenders are networked across the country and are regulated by the Small Business Association (SBA). Under this program, the SBA makes funds available to nonprofit community-based lenders (intermediaries) who, in turn, make loans available to eligible borrowers in amounts up to a maximum of $35,000. The average loan size is about $10,500. Lenders will examine your credit, your business experience, and your plan for repaying the loan. Each intermediary lender is required to provide business-based training and technical assistance to its borrowers. Individuals and small businesses applying for microloan financing may be required to fulfill training and/or planning requirements before a loan application is considered.

Barter your talents. Assess what services or products you can swap for a service or product you really need. For example, if you're starting a landscaping/lawnmowing service and need a place to park your truck or van, offer to provide your service in exchange for a parking spot in someone else's driveway or lot. You may be able to make arrangements with a local paper to provide your service to the publisher in exchange for advertising space.

Advertise for cash. Surprising, maybe. But plenty of successful entrepreneurs raised money for their endeavors this way. Check out the Business Opportunities section of your local paper for ideas on how to word your classified ads.

Structure an equity deal. In this type of deal, an investor becomes a shareholder in your new venture. The bright side is you won't show debt on your balance sheet, but be forewarned: Besides a share of profits, this person may want to become involved on the management and operations sides of your company. Are you willing to surrender some creative control?

Apply for a Small Business Association loan. Most good plans get funded. You'll need to have a written business plan that demonstrates your market research and spells out who will buy your product/service, what your costs are, etc. Take a class or get help to write the plan. There are many great classes run for free by the SBA, Small Business Development Centers, Women Business Centers, and other nonprofit organizations.

Hit up your friends/family. If a friend or relative grants you a loan, understand that he or she will want updates as to how your business is doing. Don't just take their money and run. Put together a written agreement that states exactly how much you've borrowed, how and when you intend to pay it back, and whether interest will accrue.

Lease equipment. You can borrow money for machinery and vehicles of all sorts, but beware of the interest rates for such deals and solidify a repayment plan before considering this option. Most funding sources allow for a six-month, no-payment period before any money is owed.

Try your luck. There are contests launched every day with cash prizes for lucky winners. In fact, many professional organizations, business magazines, and venture capital groups sponsor business plan competitions and photography, writing, or advertising contests. You've got to be in it to win it!

Money doesn't grow on trees, but it is out there waiting to be harvested. In the same way that students can find grant money and scholarships, you too can uncover cash that is waiting to be put to good use.

Venturing Out

In the early stages of a new venture, asking others to loan you money can be a daunting task. Being financially indebted to a friend or family member can become burdensome on your relationship. Fortunately, the venture capital (VC) industry is alive and well. A venture fund's primary goal is to achieve a significant return on its investment, either by steering a company to its initial public offering (IPO) or, unlike regular investors who are in it for the long haul, selling it within several years.

Traditionally, VCs were regarded as financing resources for start-up companies during their initial stage of growth. Today, VC funding comes in the form of equity and/or debt to companies at almost any stage of business. "This is not about passive money. This is more about bringing on someone you can trust for advice," said Scott Rechler, president and CEO of Reckson Associates Realty Corp., of Melville, New York. Since joining the company in 1989, he has overseen in excess of $2.5 billion in acquisitions and developments.

To maximize the potential of the firms they invest in, and to gain their own competitive advantage, many VCs are expanding the services they provide. Aside from financial backing, some industrialists may offer "intellectual" capital in the form of a technology officer, an enterprise development group that concentrates on executing the "next steps" of a company's business plan, and/or an advisory board, which can help guide an investment strategy appropriately.

When researching potential VCs for your business, it's important to assess how similar your business is with the other types of companies in a VC's portfolio. You should also investigate how much added value a VC can offer. For example, "By leveraging the customer base from a combined network of partners, you can cut deals and distribution agreements to mitigate the risk of any one company's success," Rechler said.

However, to be a successful venture capital fundraiser, you must be resourceful, well networked, and armed with the "chutzpah" to perfect your pitch. If you have the guts to seek out potential investors, you increase your chances of achieving glory.

There are some sure-fire do's and don'ts to pitching to a VC group:

- *Do* have a well-thought-out business plan. Investors want to determine how big your opportunity is and whether you are targeting a legitimate size market.
- *Do* spell out how you will be different from existing businesses,

and who your competitors are. It's also helpful to attach an easy-to-follow PowerPoint presentation to your plan.

- *Don't* misread your audience. Research your target investors and understand their backgrounds and interests. At a minimum you should know whether they are technologists, investment bankers, successful entrepreneurs, or trust fund beneficiaries.

You're sure to gain Brownie points if your plan includes a list of current investors and credible advisors. If people with industry credibility are already on board, it demonstrates that you've already sold your idea to someone. If your company has been unsuccessful at landing a VC, take a step back and figure out if there is something wrong with your model. If there is not a big enough market to warrant your demands, you might need to find a way to broaden it.

If you don't regularly hobnob with VCs, join networking groups to provide contact-building opportunities. If your pitch is rejected, don't take it personally and don't get discouraged. Realize that much of being successful at raising money is getting to the right person at the right time.

Touched by an Angel

Drumming up the idea for a quality project is usually the fun part of the creative process. It's the financing that's tough, unless of course you find an "angel investor"—someone who might not normally be in the investment game, but who spots your talent. Such high-net-worth individuals typically invest in entrepreneurial companies during their germination stage. Like institutional venture capital firms, many angel investors provide cash to young companies and take equity in return. One difference is that angel investors typically invest smaller amounts of money in individual companies than venture capitalists do, making them a possible resource for companies that have exhausted their "friends and family" financing options but are not ready to approach VCs for capital. Some angel investors are members of angel groups, allowing them to increase their access to investment opportunities and giving them the possibility of investing jointly with other angels to hedge their risk. Tapping into these networks is one way to start looking for investors.

Bear in mind: An angel investor is usually someone who has business experience as well as money and will probably want to play some sort of active role in managing the company. Therefore, before you accept a dime, it's important to be very clear about what he or she is bringing to the table besides money and to develop an understanding of how much creative control they expect.

These individuals are also looking for a higher rate of return than would be given by more traditional investments. Typically they expect to get 25 percent or more of their original investment.

Making It All Add Up

Many budding entrepreneurs are easily intimidated by the financial aspects of setting up a new business. However, don't despair if you don't hold a degree in accounting and haven't done long division by hand since the fourth grade. While it's natural to feel intimidated by the bookkeeping that will go along with setting up a new business, don't let this shortcoming hold you back. You don't need to be a numbers genius or even hire an accountant in order to set up your bookkeeping system. Just invest in a basic accounting software program or sign up for a free bookkeeping class on the subject through your local SCORE or other nonprofit small business group.

Good entrepreneurs quickly learn how to be resourceful. If you can't afford a computer, fax, or copier machine right away, pay a visit to your local library or Kinko's. If you need to store your product somewhere, perhaps a nearby school has a vacant room for rent. Rather than renting a whole office, maybe you can find someone who has a small corner that you can run your business out of. Many office buildings rent shared office space with access to office equipment and even secretarial support.

Living the Dream

Rich Prafder, pool cleaner turned recording artist

From the time he first picked up the saxophone at age eleven, Rich Prafder identified with the poignant lyrics of reggae music and cultivated his talent while practicing to songs of Bob Marley. But unlike many musicians who support themselves gig to gig, Prafder chose a different path to success. During high school, he built a seasonal swimming pool maintenance business, knowing it would afford him the time and money to invest in himself and in his music. Each winter, Prafder traveled to the Caribbean, where he nurtured his gift and defined his style. In order to raise money to record an album, Prafder approached one of his pool customers, whom he knew had previously invested in recording artists. "After hearing a demo tape, my backer was impressed with our passion and the refreshing new sound we'd created. Following a couple of meetings, he felt I wouldn't take no for an answer and agreed to fund our venture. Within four years, our band's debut album, *Kingston Sessions*, was completed and ready for release." The CD received positive praise and media reviews by industry opinion leaders.

A Franchise for Success?

If you want to be in business for yourself, but not by yourself, consider owning a franchise. According to the International Franchise Association (IFA), as of 2003, there were about 1,400 franchise companies based in the United States, operating a total of almost one million franchise business units. Their revenue accounts for 4 percent of the gross domestic product, according to Don Debolt, president of IFA.

What distinguishes this investment opportunity from an individually owned business is that as a franchisee, you can sell products and services with instant trademark and brand recognition. But like any other investment, purchasing a franchise is still a risk. When selecting a franchise, Mr. Debolt recommends that you carefully consider the pros and cons.

Do the research

First of all, question the demand for the product or service, and assess what the competition is like. Is there a demand for the franchiser's products or services in your community? Is the demand seasonal? Is there likely to be a continuing demand for the products or services in the future?

Does the product or service generate repeat business? How many franchised and company-owned outlets does the franchiser have in your area? How many competing companies sell the same or similar products or services? Do they offer the same goods and services at the same or lower price?

It takes blood, sweat, and tears to succeed. Some people think that a franchise operation is a turnkey business. In other words, one where the owner doesn't have to do anything. This isn't true, and that's a big reason why some franchises fail. You can't have unrealistic expectations, inadequate capital, or a lack of passion or commitment to the business. It's not a soft option, either. Forty-hour weeks are also a myth, particularly in the start-up phase of any business—it is more like sixty- to seventy-hour weeks. You must also be willing to mop floors, empty garbage, fire employees, and handle upset customers.

Consult with a franchise attorney. Besides specialized advice and guidance, he or she can help you comb through the Uniform Franchise Offering Circular (FOC). Typically provided by your franchiser, the disclosure document governs your relationship with the franchiser for the term of the contract. It also contains the franchise agreement that you will sign, defines your territory, and reveals whether you can resell your business to anyone or offer your franchiser the right of first refusal. It also identifies the executives of the franchise system, their business backgrounds, and any prior litigation against them.

What will it cost? By paying a franchise fee ($10K–$35K on average), you are provided an operating system or format developed by the company or "franchiser," the right to use the franchiser's name for a limited time, and ongoing training, advertising, and marketing support. In addition, you'll owe royalties of between 4 and 7 percent of your weekly or monthly sales. And you may be mandated to contribute to an advertising/marketing fund, too (usually 3 percent of sales).

Do your homework. The FOC should contain a listing of all the franchise owners. Before buying in, contact at least fifteen to twenty current or former franchisees. Inquire about their experience with the franchise. Did the franchiser follow through on responsibilities? Did the franchisees receive adequate training? Would they buy the franchise again? Is the business profitable? What advice would they offer you?

It can take at least a year or two before achieving a positive bottom line. So plan on reserving a financial cushion to help get you through. You will need enough money to not only open your franchise, but to run it until it is profitable.

Selling out

If you believe your business or service is outstanding, could it be a candidate for a franchise? You'll need to evaluate its merits based on certain criteria. It needs to be a highly credible business. Does it have experienced management? A track record over time? Is the concept proven? Has it achieved good local press or public acclaim? It needs to be unique. Can it be differentiated from competitors? Is it marketable as a business opportunity? Does it have a sustainable competitive advantage?

Living the Dream

Jeni Garrett, CEO, Woodhouse Day Spas Corp.

This twenty-five-year-old cost accountant turned entrepreneur used to savor the facials and body treatments she'd sometimes treat herself to. Now she owns one of the fastest growing day-spa franchises in America. Jeni and her husband combined their business instincts with their love of historic architecture and opened the first Woodhouse Day Spa in Victoria, Texas, in 2001. "We enjoy restoring landmark homes. The ambiance is conducive to relaxation and our renovations upgrade the community," explained Jeni.

By fourth quarter, 2004, Woodhouse will expand to include thirteen nationwide locations, from Pennsylvania to Nashville. "Our five-year goal is to have 200 units," Jeni said.

The company offers seventy different treatments and carries highly exclusive retail products, as well as their own private-label natural and organic product line.

While franchising came naturally to her, Jeni has learned a thing or two about this unique business system. "We pulled in an incredible franchise attorney and quality control officer right away. You need the right specialists in place from the get-go. And we've been very selective with our franchisees. They have to share our vision, which is to help change people's lives. We won't sell it to someone who's just in it for the money," said Jeni.

If you're interested in becoming a Woodhouse Spa franchisee, the start-up investment costs run from $153,000 to $268,000.

It needs to be teachable. Are the systems in place? Are operating procedures documented? Could someone learn to operate the business in three months or less?

It needs to provide an adequate return—and that's not just profitability. If a business cannot generate a 15 to 20 percent return on investment after deducting a royalty (typically between 4 and 8 percent), it is going to be difficult to keep your franchisees happy.

The Top Franchises for Creative Types

Here are some names of the many companies offering franchise opportunities that will allow you to not only make money but stay in touch with your creative side.

Candy Bouquet—*www.candybouquet.com.* Specializes in floral-like creations crafted from gourmet chocolates and candies. Start-up: $7.3K–$44.1K.

City Looks Salons International—(952) 947-7328. Full-service, upscale hair salon chain. Start-up: $95K–$172K.

Complete Music—*www.cmusic.com.* Mobile DJ entertainment service. Start-up: $19.7K–$33K.

Computertots/Computer Explorers—*www.computertots.com.* Computer classes for young children. Start-up: $32.1K–$48.5K.

Curves—*www.buycurves.com.* Women's fitness and weight-loss centers. Start-up: $30K–$36K.

Deck the Walls—*www.dtwfraninfo.com.* Specializes in art, wall décor, and custom framing. Each store offers a wide selection of limited edition prints, preframed art, custom framing moldings, and mat styles. Start-up: $45K–$80K.

Drama Kids International, Inc.—*www.dramakids.com.* After-school children's drama programs. Start-up costs: $33.4K–$39K.

Furniture Medic—*www.furnituremedicfranchise.com.* Furniture restoration and repair service. Start-up: $35.5K–$78.9K.

Great Wraps!—*www.greatwraps.net.* Wrapped sandwich

franchise. Features a full line of wraps, burritos, cheese steaks, and smoothies. Start-up: $175K–$275K.

Happy & Healthy Products, Inc.—*www.fruitfull.com.* Frozen fruit bars and smoothies. Start-up: $23K–$55K.

IM= X Pilates Studio—*www.xercize.com.* Pilates instructor certification and patented Pilates equipment sales and development. Helps customers grow Pilates programs. Start-up: $18K–$30K.

Interiors by Decorating Den—*www.decoratingden.com.* Interior decorating services and products. Start-up: $40K.

Kabloom—*www.kabloom.com.* Floral retailer with warm, inviting, fun stores and a large selection of the freshest flowers and plants. Start-up: $150K.

KidzArt—*www.kidzart.com.* An enrichment program of inspiring drawing lessons and art projects for kids and for adults who want to reexperience the joy of art. Start-up: $14.9K–$21K.

Lil' Angels Photography—Preschool and day-care photography. Start-up: $27K–$32K.

Merle Norman Cosmetics—*www.merlenorman.com.* Cosmetics studios. Start-up: $33.1K–$162K.

Outdoor Connection—*www.outdoor-connection.com.* Fishing and hunting trips. Start-up: $10.4K–$15.1K.

The Sports Section—*www.sports-section.com.* Youth and sports photography. Start-up: $17.2K–$52.7K.

Stretch-N-Grow International, Inc.—*www.stretch-n-grow. com.* On-site children's fitness programs. Start-up: $15K–$20K.

Tropical Smoothie Café—*www.tropicalsmoothie.com.* Committed to helping people lead healthy lives. Serves products to create the ultimate experience in quick, casual dining. Start-up: $40K–$50K.

The Visual Image, Inc.—*www.thevisualimageinc.com.* Preschool and pet photography. Start-up: $37.3K–$37.5K.

Woodhouse Spas Corp.—*www.woodhousespas.com.* Day spa offers seventy different treatments and carries several lines of highly exclusive retail products, including skin care, bath and body products, aromatherapy, home essentials, and specialty products. Startup: $153,750–$254,625.

It Takes Two

Perhaps in your case, two heads (and bank accounts) would be better than one for starting your side business. But how can you guarantee that the partner you choose will be a good match? In reality—you can't.

Often, the rules of dating mirror those of the business world. Never commit to anything on the first meeting. Your courtship should be long enough to get to know a potential partner. And always weigh the costs and benefits of getting into bed together. While new business partnerships are formed every day, it takes caution, clear objectives, and complimentary skill sets for relationships to prosper and last.

Before you decide whether or not to take someone on as a business partner, realize that not every friendship or family tie is designed to go commercial. There are some basic rules for protecting your camaraderie.

Communicate regularly

First, find a trustworthy collaborator. Make sure you know this person well and that both of you have a clear understanding of how your responsibilities are divided up. Who is president? Who makes the hiring decisions? Even if your offices are in different buildings, agree to meet for lunch at least once a week and remain in constant dialogue via e-mail and phone.

Sign a partnership agreement

Among other things, this document spells what options you have if one of you should happen to want out of the business, go bankrupt, die, or divorce. It's meant to protect you as well as your company, family, and spouse. Make sure your cohort is in this for the long haul, or be sure to delineate an exit strategy for yourself.

Living the Dream

Rachel Isaac, etchings artist

Some people can look close to home for a business partner. For Pennsylvania-based artist Rachel Isaac, mom, Joanne, serves as her mentor, emotional support, and business ally. "When I got out of college, my mother wanted me to work for her in her studio. But I knew I'd get lost in that relationship and that it would be hard to carve out my own identity. To maintain a degree of separation, Rachel and Joanne work out of different studios and each handles her own bookkeeping. The two work together at trade shows, splitting the drive time and financial costs of exhibiting, ordering materials, and shipping their artwork. Since Rachel's studio doubles as a framing gallery, she is also able to service her mother's customers. "We talk every day about business matters and share new techniques," Rachel said. For her, the experience, contacts, and reputation of her mother have been invaluable. "She's really blazed a trail," said Rachel. "She never followed other artists. She created her own style and never went along with anyone else's rules." Rachel and Joanne exhibit annually at the Philadelphia Flower Show, the world's largest indoor exhibition of its kind.

Define your responsibilities

Perhaps one of you is more capable in strategic planning, marketing, and sales, while the other shines at public relations and graphic design. Having a clear division of duties will help you to maximize your unique strengths.

Living the Dream

Julian Niccolini and Alex von Bidder, managing partners,
The Four Seasons Restaurant

Julian Niccolini and his partner, Alex von Bidder, met at the landmark Four Seasons restaurant in the 1970s. "The former owners hired us with an eye toward grooming us to one day take over," said Julian. "They believed that if we both had expertise in different sets of restaurant skills, we'd never be jealous of each other and would work better together. Julian and Alex's partnership works in part due to their great chemistry. "We are completely supportive of each other because we are not in competition. I worry about details. Alex is a big picture person." However, there is always an upside and downside of a joint venture. "Alex and I both got lucky. I have heard of partnerships where one person does all the work and starts to resent the less motivated partner." Julian gives some words of caution for anyone contemplating partnering with a pal or relative. "Be careful. By going into a partnership with a close friend or family member, you run the risk of destroying relationships. My friendship with Alex grew from our partnership. I am not sure if it would have worked so well if our partnership grew from a friendship. It is far easier to be friends with a partner than to be partners with a friend."

Above all, resolve disputes quickly

Don't let issues fester and undermine your personal and professional partnership. Events such as a new product launch or downsizing can cause tension between you and your partner. If you both have different views on how to handle such situations, try to use constructive, not offensive criticism. If you need to let go of frustration, walk away from each other and take a time-out. Take a deep breath and get some silence. Try not to talk shop after hours—give each other a chance to breathe and be regular people. Plus, your friends and family will appreciate your undivided attention.

Summary

Don't be put off just because you're new to being in business. Lots of first-time businesses are a success, and yours need not be any different, but you do have to do your homework.

Tips to remember:

- Make sure you have a plan to keep the cash coming in, especially in the critical start-up phase.
- Uncover every stone when raising capital for your business. Think outside the box when it comes to raising money.
- Look into ways of starting up that can give you emotional and financial support, such as franchising options or going into business with a partner.

Chapter 5

Freedom Fighting:
Negotiate the Flexibility You Need
to Pursue Your Passion

Did you know that Americans waste an average of two to four work hours each day on time-stealing culprits such as Web surfing and unimportant paperwork? Imagine how much more rewarding your work life could be if you redirected this passive energy toward a parallel job or income.

If you feel stuck and purposeless in your current work environment, don't wait until your life becomes one big panic attack. Reexamine the behavior patterns that govern how you budget your time. For example, perhaps you regularly take on extra work assignments to appease management. Ask yourself, how much are the Brownie points you're scoring with your boss really worth? What about your physical and mental health? Is your candle burning out at both ends? If you add up all the pockets of time that you allow other forces to consume your attention, you may be surprised at how many nonreturnable minutes you forfeit on a regular basis. Learn to say no to duties beyond your core job description. Make your happiness and well-being your top priorities. Reclaim your personal time and devote it to creating your ideal work and lifestyle.

Living the Dream

Tanya Clarke, actress/masseuse

At one time, actress Tanya Clarke was playing the real-life role of a starving artist.

The Canadian native arrived in Manhattan, New York, fresh out of high school, to follow her dream of working as an actress. However, she quickly found herself working as a waitress at local diners just to survive. "I was living on roughly $300 a week, at one point sharing living expenses with eight roommates in a two-bedroom apartment. Someone was actually living in our closet. I hit an emotional rock bottom and decided to shift my attention to another long-term interest—massage. With income from my work in commercials, I completed a fifteen-month program at New York's Swedish Institute. Today, I have a thriving private client base. I create my own hours and pursue film and theatrical projects in my free time, including a bit part in the box office hit *A Beautiful Mind*. No longer financially unstable, I have much more confidence now. I'm not constantly desperate when I walk into an audition. I can approach acting as something I want to do because I love it. I'm optimistic that my "big break" will come, but I don't dwell on it. I'm not putting my whole focus on it. I put that focus on my clients in a positive way. I enjoy making them feel good."

Independence Days: Careers with Flexible Hours

Are you holding down a menial, unrewarding job that barely pays the bills? You don't have to wait tables or pump gas while trying to make your dreams true. There are plenty of jobs that are both stimulating and well paid and won't interfere with your creative activities or side business.

Freelance journalist/writer
Realtor
Dog groomer
Music tutor
Masseuse
Fitness instructor
Accountant
Web site developer
Caterer
Graphic designer
Child-care provider
Grant writer
Electronic publicist
Cosmetics salesperson
Personal trainer
Bartender
Makeup artist

Free Your Spirit

Just how adaptable are you willing to be in order to realize your passion? Can you quit your job, relocate, and attempt to pursue your creative ambition? Probably not, and that is precisely why very few people are living their most authentic lives. Others have weighed the risks and rewards of leading a life that doesn't allow them to pursue their passions wholeheartedly and have opted against it. To drive their ideas, they keep their minds and options open.

Following your true nature may entail veering off the beaten path and risking what's safe and habitual. Artistic people often need to take risks, live on the edge, or tread unfamiliar territory in order to fuel and exercise their talents. Don't hold yourself back out of fear or self-doubt. You may need to break out of the corporate mold and live on the bare necessities for a while in order to heed your artistic calling. But remind yourself that life is filled with unknowns. If you close yourself off from growth opportunities, you'll never know what could have been.

Living the Dream

Michael Weintraub, celebrity photographer

As a young boy, Michael Weintraub was obsessed with rock concerts. Determined to work in the music industry someday, the self-taught photographer learned how to finagle his way into events and built up quite a portfolio of the musicians he'd captured on film. "I would call magazines to learn which performers they were doing upcoming stories on. I'd convince them to put in a press pass request for me at festivals and shows where the artists were slated to perform. Slowly I built up quite a portfolio of published clips." His valuable collection includes music legends like Ray Charles, Bono, and Al Green. Today, this sole proprietor licenses his copyrighted images to top music publications such as *Rolling Stone* and *Downbeat* for extra income. But living a dream doesn't always equal dreamy living. While he earns roughly $40,000 a year, his freelance work style doesn't include health-insurance benefits and can be quite isolating. Still, at age twenty-eight, this rising star in the music photography world is enjoying his nomadic lifestyle. "I'd like more money coming in, but that will come. I'm living my dream right now. I believe in leaving yourself open to possibilities."

All for Your Benefit

In our hyperfast business world, it isn't easy to balance work and a personal life. But flexible work options can significantly ease the struggle. Choosing part-time hours, job sharing, or a compressed work week can help you understand your values and goals, set realistic expectations, take better care of yourself, and make changes in your life.

Since quality of life has become a chief priority for today's workers, corporate America is reacting to this trend by hiring work/life professionals, who are trained to educate businesses, support employees in their daily juggling act, and ultimately improve an organization's bottom line.

For employers, the attraction of work/life balance programs centers on recruiting and retention issues, according to Stephanie Trapp, executive director of The Alliance of Work/Life Professionals, a national trade organization. "Employers are creating attractive benefit packages to better meet the needs of their employees in order to have them remain with their company," she said. The results of such policies often include fewer missed meetings, less distractions, increased productivity, and more loyalty.

Some of the more groundbreaking work/life programs include on-site schooling and summer camp, in-house fitness clubs, lactation rooms, eldercare referral services, paternity leave, power napping, concierge services, ergonomically sound work spaces, and even corporate-sponsored cooking lessons that encourage families to make the time to eat together.

Remote Control

Another way to create more independence for yourself, without giving up your steady income, is by telecommuting. Under this work-from-home arrangement, you can tackle your workload at your own pace and reserve a portion of your day for side work. Plus, this modern work style will save you money in travel expenses and aggravation from traffic nightmares. "People spend an average of $17,000 in owning and operating their cars annually," said Edward McNally, director of marketing and communications for the Metro Atlanta

Chamber of Commerce. "If you put that into your mortgage, you could afford a much bigger home," he said.

Telecommuting, or being able to spend some of your work life at home, offers a whole new kind of flexibility, but there are rules to making this arrangement work. Some employers are wary and even downright suspicious of work-from-home arrangements or flexible hours. You need to make them and other coworkers feel comfortable with it.

1. *Always be on time with your work.* This may mean picking up the slack from other departments in order to make your commitments. Don't be rigid about your job description, and also, don't let others let you down.

2. *Have a good work ethic.* That means that if you need to meet a deadline, you must be prepared to work long, unsociable hours and holidays. In return, you are free to make up the time elsewhere.

3. *Be low maintenance.* Do your job without fussing, fighting, and feuding. Your work should appear as if by magic and, where possible, need little involvement from others.

4. *Never get involved in office infighting or politics.* You are able to work outside it, so don't get dragged into it. And if you are not there to defend yourself, you could find yourself being the patsy.

5. *Do face time in the office.* While you need to be low-key, you shouldn't be invisible. Make sure supervisors are aware you are at your job and not sloping off for an unscheduled vacation.

6. *Be reachable at all times by e-mail and cell phone.* Check your messages and reply to them as promptly as possible. If people at the office have a hard time getting to you, they will get frustrated and suspicious.

7. *Always be available for meetings and conference calls.* You can afford to accommodate others' time frames, so unless there is a crucial clash, make it easy for them.

8. *Make sure people know when you are taking official vacation.* Don't let that blend into your everyday work. Otherwise, if you are away and not returning calls, you will be considered slovenly. Since the down side of flexible hours is that you are often never actually OFF the clock, switch the cell phone off and relax!

If others in your company are overworked or overburdened, offer to help them out where you can. If you breeze out of the office at 2:00 P.M. while they are there until the late evening hours, resentment will form. You may have commitments that mean you have to leave at 2:00, and that's okay, but offer to take some of their work home or unburden them from a task you can do for them another time. If your coworkers like you, they will be less prone to jealousy or resentment.

If you haven't a second to spend on yourself at the end of your workday, you may be caught in an excessively inflexible work environment. If your employer is reluctant to adopt a formal work-life program, consider switching to a job with a more supportive and accommodating culture.

Invest in Yourself

If you're itching to climb to the next notch on your employer's ladder or a lack of education is holding you back from pursuing a more desirable job or side business, consider attending an online college. Being able to do classes from your home may provide you the extra time and flexibility you need to continue your education.

Each year, about 40 percent of our nation's adult population participates in some form of formal instruction, according to a recent study published by the University Continuing Education

Association (UCEA). During tough economic times, people return to school in higher numbers to become more saleable in the marketplace. Given the competitive job market and unstable stock market, it's easy to understand why 46,000 students pursued a higher degree at The University of Phoenix Online. "Enrollments grew 80 percent in 2001," according to Brian Mueller, CEO. "We live in an ambitious culture. People want to participate at higher levels."

Living the Dream

Elizabeth Griffiths, virtual manager, Prodigy Communications

Based out of the Internet service provider's Austin, Texas, headquarters, Griffiths "virtually" manages fifty independent contractors, each of whom serves as a community leader for online interest groups with titles such as "Gardening" and "Crafts and Hobbies."

Griffiths says that patience and communication are key traits for a virtual manager, while time management is a crucial skill. "I'm keenly aware of the unique tribulations of this modern work option. While telecommuters enjoy the independence of working on their own time, one criticism of such freedom is the opportunity to slack off. However, I can ensure that my leaders are doing what their contract calls for. For example, Web pages are supposed to be updated twice a week. I can access their file transfer protocol (FTP) directories, which show how and when they're uploading. To build morale, I hold evening and weekend chats with my leaders in cyberspace. It would be great to have the face-to-face contact, but it doesn't impact their job or mine in the least. One of the qualities I look for in a leader is a level of independence. I encourage them to be where the buck stops.

Whatever your interest, at any stage of life, continuing education offers more flexibility and choices than ever before. While such schooling is an expense, the return on investment often far outweighs the price individuals pay. As we move into the twenty-first century, "distance learning" will persist as a trend in continuing education. Virtually every American home has access to some sort of instructional technology, including the Internet, video, and audio tapes. The ability to study at your own pace within your own home is an option that works for many people and may work for you as well—particularly if you're juggling a full-time job. Today, a wide variety of online credit and noncredit courses exist for undergrads and graduates, including certificates in online selling, importing and exporting, direct marketing, graphic design, and figure drawing.

Increasing your education is one of the smartest investments you can make as you strive toward a more personally and financially rewarding work life. By advancing your knowledge base, training, and skills, you can capitalize on your creative assets and ease the transition.

Summary

Finding flexibility in your current work life can give you the perfect opportunity to try other directions before branching out entirely. You may find you can coexist very well this way and need never give up your primary source of income. Getting to a good place within your current job is key to being able to negotiate for that kind of work set-up.

Tips to remember:

- Look at the different ways you can perform your job that will give you the most freedom. Perhaps telecommuting will work for you or part-time hours or days.

- Going back to school could be just what your career needs, and by the same token, you can also use flexible options to make this happen. Consider part-time or online learning to help you achieve your goals.

Living the Dream

Mary Jane Williams, contracts administrator/virtual student

As a contracts administrator for an aerospace company, Ms. Williams was told by her supervisor that to be promoted to a management role, she'd need to get an undergraduate degree in business. Though she was ready to head back to school and her employer was prepared to reimburse her for the full tuition costs, this working mother viewed her frequent business travel as an obstacle. She surfed the Web in search of an online college that would meet her needs and discovered Kaplan College. Impressed with their course descriptions, Ms. Williams enrolled herself in their bachelor of science program in applied management. Though she's never personally met any of her twenty virtual classmates, she joins them each week in cyberspace for real-time seminars on subjects such as accounting and management. The classes are set up like chat rooms, where professors and students can instant message each other. Students are given weekly reading assignments and quizzed online to test their understanding of the material. For their final exam, they must write an extensive paper. "As a working parent, it would have been difficult to go back to college. Now I work toward my degree at my own pace, and I don't have to be away from my family."

Chapter 6

Home Sweet Home:
It Can Also Be the Best Place to Work

If you are a housewife, house husband, stay-at-home mom or dad, or caretaker for other family members as your full-time occupation, then pursuing your creative goals brings on a whole new set of difficulties. First, you have different time and energy management needs. Second, since you may not be contributing financially toward the household budget, spending money on your new goals may not be possible.

The good news is that whether you're underemployed, underchallenged, or in need of extra income, there are more home-based business opportunities today than ever before. More folks are discovering that it's possible to turn their bread-winning ideas into money *and* keep their family relationships intact.

Working Against the Biological Clock

It's hard to imagine a time when the biological clock ruled the female life cycle. These days, it seems the clock most working women adhere to is the one they use to punch in and out of work with. Today, the median age for a woman bearing her first child is 24.3, according to *Working Mother* magazine. Even at this early stage of a woman's career, it is important for her to plan and set herself up for motherhood—and achieve enough to take a break if she desires.

Picking the right mate and developing a work/life strategy

very early on are the keys to having it all, according to Joan K. Peters, author of *Not Your Mother's Life: Changing the Rules of Work, Love, and Family* (Perseus Books). Before becoming, say, a stock analyst, formulate a mental picture of what your life will look like. "Don't just look at the work, but at how people in the field live their lives. Do they work 60 hours per week? Do hours ebb and flow? What is the lifestyle of people in a chosen field? Are success or promotions incumbent upon minimal family life or frequent travel? Consider the spiritual as well as the monetary currency of your choice," Peters advises.

If you've been resisting your maternal instincts to have a baby, take comfort in knowing that young working women have much greater flexibility today than at any other time in history. While you'll never be 100 percent ready for the transition to motherhood, you don't have to stop achieving in your career or pursuing your creative dream. You need to decide what "quality of life" means to you, according to Hilary Boyd, author of *Working Woman's Pregnancy* (Mitchell Beazley). Working women on the verge of becoming first-time moms have to address many practical issues.

Many new moms face separation anxiety. Being anxious as you reenter the workplace or begin a creative endeavor and turn your baby over to a caregiver is natural. You may feel guilty about working, a natural reaction when your caregiver tells you about your baby's first step or if you're not around to comfort her when she's sick. Don't fight this feeling. Instead, view the time you do have together as precious, and don't fret about the parts you're absent for.

After a long day on the job, you may be too exhausted to feed, bathe, or play with your child. Communicate and share such tasks with your partner. Or pay your caregiver to stay overtime so that you can unwind before resuming your parenting duties.

You may find you need a rest from your career or business. If economic circumstances permit, consider taking a sabbatical, reducing your work hours, or switching to a seasonal or part-time job. You'll feel rejuvenated and learn how to manage your work and family life more effectively.

Living the Dream

Karen Adams, "mompreneur"

Beginning at age twenty-three, Karen Adams built, acquired, and sold several technology companies before deciding to "retire" to care for her two young daughters. "I went from being a twelve-hour-a-day workaholic to being a stay-at-home mom by age twenty-nine," she recalled. But the business bug soon bit again. From all the time spent in her children's rooms, "I realized that there weren't a lot of good kids furnishing resources out there." The timing was right for her brainchild, an upscale online baby and children's furniture store. Today, PoshTots is a multimillion-dollar, privately held company that employs a full-time staff of twenty. Karen's success now extends to her work/life balancing act. I handle various projects that allow me to work outside the corporate office," she explained. Karen typically works from 8:00 A.M. to 2:30 P.M., when her kids return from school. Once they're asleep, she resumes computer work. At age thirty-four, Karen admits she's taken an evolutionary approach to being a mom and CEO. "You can have it all, but what you define that as before you have kids is not how you're going to define it after you have kids. It's a process of structuring your career and how that relates to your new family life . . . and experimenting with that balance," she said.

Having a dream and pursuing it is a very noble concept, but when your home and family life suffers because of it, then it can become a big problem. It need not be this way. With discipline, careful planning, family support, and help from professional services, you can master the work/family juggling act without sacrificing your desires. For example, ask for help with household chores when necessary, set time limits to work on your project, involve your family (when possible) in your business pursuits, and shower your loved ones with niceties when you eventually earn some cash from your venture.

Mom's the Word

Our country's work-life movement stems from the 26 million (and growing) working mothers out there today. Therefore, the most popular work/life initiative today is daycare, in its many forms. There are in-house and corporate-subsidized child-care options, nanny referral services, and even on-site nurses.

If you don't think your company's benefit plan stacks up to one of modern-day caliber, there are steps you can take to improve it, from organizing task forces to conducting employee-wide surveys. "There are a lot of grass roots efforts that can help to bring about change," said Jean Holbrook, director of product management for Lifeworks, a division of the Ceridian Corporation, a payroll and human resources support company. In more cases than not, "The bottom line makes such benefits programs appear worthwhile. For every dollar a company spends, it probably saves $4 in recruitment costs and employee absenteeism," she added.

Even smaller companies can structure such plans—the key is creativity. While it may not be cost effective to develop on-site child-care, such firms can reach out to their local business community and negotiate lower rates or vouchers for daycare providers on their employees' behalf. Work with your human resources representative to see if these might be options your company can explore.

Perking Up: How Employers Keep Family-Minded Workers Happy

There are several incentives that companies are offering new moms to make sure they don't leave the company. One is lactation rooms.

New moms have a private space where they can continue to breast-feed after returning to work. Sometimes companies will even foot the bill for a lactation expert, who provides counseling before and after a woman is ready to reenter her workplace.

On-site summer camp is a great help for families. When school lets out for vacation or holidays, most parents scramble to schedule activities that will keep their children occupied. When such plans fail, many employees end up unexpectedly taking off from work to provide supervision. Employers are recognizing that an on-site facility keeps their workers on site, too. Having a summer camp or holiday program in effect or contracting with a local camp is well worth the return on investment.

To counter the productivity drain stemming from employees who are dealing with attending to their aging parents, companies are starting to extend elder-care referral services. Such agencies can help employees select an assisted-living facility or conduct a needs assessment of care.

In-house fitness clubs or discounted memberships to the local gym are common wellness benefits. But some of the more nontraditional offerings today include on-site flu shots, yoga instruction, chair massage, and weight-loss counseling, all of which are important for busy parents who lack the time to deal with these things.

Creative Home Businesses

If you're limited to staying at home for family reasons, you have to be even more careful when it comes to choosing a creative sideline. The chances are it can't entail too much start-up cost or need a lot of space or special equipment. However, there are plenty of opportunities out there.

Antique restorer

Share your passion for all things old by becoming an antique furniture restorer/finisher. Work consists of repairing antique furniture by replacing missing or broken parts and finishing or refinishing furniture. You can start your own small business or be contracted out to antique dealers. You should possess artistic and technical skills, as well as business skills in money management and communication.

Interior designer

If you have a passion for decorating a home, you could become an interior designer. Business is booming today for the home-fixing professions. In fact, the Department of Labor projects that by 2008, the number of interior design professionals will surpass 67,000, a significant increase from 1998, when there were just over 53,000.

Many people don't know where to start when they are remodeling or buying a house for the first time. If you have knowledge of colors and patterns, a flair for fabrics and finishings, plus the expertise and contacts for locating materials and furnishings, this may be the perfect home-based business for you. To educate yourself about the field and receive training in drawing work and calculating floor plans, take a course and sample the reality of the industry.

Photographer

Armed with a camera, tripod, and sufficient room for developing your photos, you can start your own photography business at home. You can choose to specialize in weddings, models, press shots, album cover photography, family portraits, passports, student photos, or local newspaper coverage. Not much equipment is necessary to get going—a camera off the store shelf can often do the trick today. Don't neglect the business side of your craft. You'll need to advertise and develop a list of clients who are willing to license your images.

Bed-and-breakfast operator

While this business can be purchased, most bed-and-breakfast businesses start out as a large house with a lot of extra rooms. Converting a house will involve expenses such as adding bathrooms. You will also have to meet local guidelines for bed and breakfasts (such as adequate escape routes in case of a fire), and you'll likely need local approval to start one. It's challenging work, but if you think of it as an extension of your usual family housework and duties, you can start a bed and breakfast in your own place. If your visitors enjoy their stay, many become repeat customers, coming back to the same familiar surroundings time and again. Realize, though, the hours can be long, and it's a business that usually runs seven days per week, fifty-two weeks a year. Finally, marketing a bed and breakfast on the Internet is very important too. Many reservations are made online, or the initial contact is through e-mail.

Babysitting/daycare

Due to the financial pressures many families face today, many parents work outside of the home to bring in enough income to pay daily living expenses. This creates a home-based opportunity. Children must be watched all day if they're not in school or for a brief time after school before the parents finish work for the day. If you enjoy children, then a home daycare may be a great option for you. You can do this at home for only a small investment in basic equipment and toys for the kids, in addition to the advertising of your business. However, make sure you check your local laws regarding licensing, and get professional advice on legalities and insurance before beginning.

Event planner

Whether it's a kids' party or a large wedding, party planners are in demand. If you loathe the idea of having to market yourself or cold-call prospects to land clients, you may want to work for a planning company rather than striking out on your own. The range of party-planning specialties is vast today: corporate picnics, cruises, conferences, fundraisers, holiday events, birthday parties—the list goes on. Bear in mind that this is not a business you can jump into overnight. Most planners are paid based upon experience and education, so build a strong portfolio and resume. If you have a day job, you might want to keep it as you build your client base.

Pet care

Professional, personalized in-home pet care at the client's house is a growth trend. This may also include dog walking, bringing in mail and newspapers, watering plants, and checking security.

Travel agent

If you enjoy travel to exotic destinations, you'll find being a deluxe travel agent extremely fulfilling. For your clients, travel tends to be culturally focused, only the finest accommodations suffice, and travelers usually fly first or business class. They seek expert guides and high-quality vehicle transportation. Such requests may include taking a cooking class given by a local chef from a particularly culinary-rich spot on the map or exploring an area known for folk art and handcrafts.

Home businesses offer plenty of perks (flexibility, casual dress, no boss, no commute, family management, and tax breaks.) However, before jumping into one, make sure it ideally suits your skills and interest. Working from home can be quiet and isolating. You may find yourself checking your e-mail constantly or wishing the phone would ring. To avoid the loneliness, try to do at least a couple of things that allow you to interact with people each day. This could mean joining a professional club or attending a trade show. Form joint ventures with other home-business services that compliment your service. If silence is anything but golden for you, turn on some background music as you work.

Creating an Inspired Home Office

If your work environment is drab and uninspiring, how can you expect your productivity and output to be anything more than mediocre at best? It's critical that you are warmed and comforted in your workspace, agrees Paul Gleicher, president of Gleicher Design Group, a Manhattan-based architecture and interior design firm.

Living the Dream

Judi Boren, owner, Posh Papers

After twenty years in business, Judi Boren should be pleased that handcrafts are back in vogue. As founder and owner of Rhode Island-based Posh Papers, Boren had a vision to create unique lines of personalized note cards that maintained a hand-drawn, custom-made look. Boren began making her special note cards for neighbors and friends. Her first design subjects (which remain top sellers today) were faces and silhouettes of elegant, fashionable ladies from the 1920s era. "I used ink, traced each one by hand, and embellished them with feathers, lace, rhinestones, lace, felt, and netting," she said.

Boren attended night school to earn an art degree and also enrolled in a commercial printing course. Today, Posh Papers operates out of Boren's home studio. The company sends out an annual sixteen-page color catalog to over 20,000 people, many of whom are wholesale accounts or repeat customers, and sometimes even celebrities such as Cicely Tyson, Dionne Warwick, and Camille Cosby. The company does over $100,000 in annual sales, half of which is generated during the Christmas holiday period. For Boren, the greatest reward of succeeding on her own terms is delighting her customers. "When people call me and tell me that everybody they gave my notes to loved them, it's a thrill," she said.

"If you're in a cold, dark, and dusty environment, it will be a downer. But when your space is vibrant and inviting, your creative juices are free to flow," he said. Whether you operate out of a cubicle or a home office, consider how to personalize and perk up your surroundings. It may well be worth the investment.

When making changes, understand your personality. Decide whether you are stimulated more by visual images and personal mementos or prefer clutter-free, Zen-like surroundings. Depending on which extreme you fall into, you may desire more pinup space for corkboards, photographs, and magazine clippings, or clear counters with only essentials at your fingertips, neatly arranged bookshelves, a miniature water fountain, personal sandbox, or an inspirational quote-of-the-day calendar.

Color your world. Bold, active shades like red tend to energize, while green is calming. You need not paint entire walls either. Add splashes of color using plants or a vase with fresh-cut flowers.

Don't skimp on your seat. If you sit for long hours at a time, invest in a well-made chair with adjustable heights (Herman Miller and Knoll are great designer bets). Your feet should lie flat on the floor and your back should be well supported to ensure you don't get fatigued.

Is your keyboard resting at the appropriate height and distance from your body? Is it time for a new, shaper computer monitor? If your job entails heavy phone and data-entry work, could you use a headset?

The most ideal light source is natural daylight. In addition, include a mix of nonglare, general, and task lighting. Position overhead lighting directly over or in front of your head so as not to cast a shadow. Studies have shown that people are more productive in natural light.

Work flow is also key to any office layout. Ideally, you should have quick and easy access to your equipment and furniture. This takes planning, sketching, and measuring. You must consider the angles of furniture in relation to windows, doors, closets, and radiators. If your office is in need of an organizational overhaul, don't panic. You don't have to take it on alone. There are handymen and outside services that specialize in professional organization. They may be worth the investment if it means you'll have a comfortable and efficient space to work in.

Staying Sane

Home workers continually have their work and family intertwined in one setting—which can be a challenge for you, your family, and your business. In order to accomplish anything in either area, you'll need to protect your work time and space through the creation of rules, boundaries, and schedules that meet your needs.

If you have a private office, for example, a closed door will indicate to your family and home workers that work is in progress. You might even want to hang an Open/Closed or Do Not Disturb sign on your office door to let your family know when you do not want to be interrupted.

Short on workspace? Utilize bookshelves and wall units to create functional and organized quarters.

Sharing a home office with a partner or significant other? You'll each need a section of wall/pinup space to call your own. Pass on the florals and chintz window coverings and instead select wooden or bamboo blinds for a more gender-neutral look.

Need privacy from other members of the household? Add panels on top of a workspace partition to create a more secluded vibe.

Afraid of becoming a homebody? E-mail or phone friends and family throughout the day to relieve stress and stay connected. Walking the dog or going out for coffee are additional ways to get out of the house for a deserved breather.

If you have young kids, separating work from family is going to be nearly impossible. You'll need to be very innovative at times in order to get any work done. To avoid having important papers ripped up or colored, objects stuck in disk drives, or fax machines jammed with toys, visualize what layout would work best for you when you are working and caring for the kids concurrently. For example, locating your office near your kitchen will make it easier to quench thirsty or snack-hungry kids. An inexpensive television and VCR will occupy your toddlers when they've tired of their toys. A small desk is ideal for crafting or pretending to help you with your work.

Lock file drawers, place office supplies high on shelves, put up safety gates to prevent kids from touching expensive computer equipment, and make sure that your blinds are safe from dangling cords and tassels.

As your business expands, your home may not offer the space you require. You may need more room for storage, business-related projects, the flow of paperwork…not to mention more workspace. When the time comes to expand, consider converting another room, adding on to your home, or putting up a separate facility to function as a warehouse.

A final reminder: You may work all of your life, but your children will only be children now. In the beginning of parenthood, you'll have to make a lot of adjustments, and your home office will be one of them. Just do what you can, work when you can, and keep in mind why you wanted to work from home in the first place.

Making Homework Pay Off

If you own a computer and a modem, it may be time to dust off your monitor and start putting your computer to work for you. Today, the PC allows you to do much more than gab online, check stock prices, and generate seasonal greeting cards. If you're computer savvy and willing to do some research, there are plenty of home-based business opportunities that you can do either full- or part-time. Putting your computer skills to work can earn you extra money or help you forge a new career or business in many creative areas.

Online public relations

With the gazillions of businesses and organizations that have developed an online presence, the competition for eyeballs is fierce.

There's a demand for tech-savvy electronic public relations personnel. These publicists can create e-press releases, pitch articles for online publications, and e-mail letters and media kits. Potential clients include high-tech firms and software manufacturers.

Medical billers

Medical billers can often work from home. In this role, you will be responsible for sending claims electronically to Medicare and health insurance companies for review and remittance. You may also invoice patients for copayments, maintain patient accounts, and follow up on rejected claims. With a doctor for every ailment, you won't have to look too hard for potential clients. You will need to invest in the appropriate software packages, though, which run between $500 and $10,000.

Internet trainers

If you know your way around a computer and are good with people, then being an Internet trainer is a great home-based business. Senior citizen groups, businesses, educational institutions, and other organizations are hiring tech experts. To market yourself, advertise in your community or regional business press. Network at your local chamber of commerce and other business organizations. Pitch yourself to Internet service providers (ISPs) in your area.

Make E-Commerce Pay

With around 7,000 new online sellers each day, the time is ripe to get your slice of e-commerce action, according to Todd Pearson, senior vice president of merchant services for Pay-Pal (*www.paypal.com*), a company that enables businesses and consumers to send and receive secure Internet payments. If you decide to sell your home-based products or services through sites such as eBay, make sure you know your trash from your treasure. Also, remember that customer service can make or break your e-business. Pay-Pal offers relationship management software tools, including e-mail management, mailing lists, instant payment notification, integrated shipping with UPS, and a transaction history Web site through which merchants can check the status of individual orders.

Living the Dream

Mike and Sharon Baker, owners, WeSellArt.com

Today this husband and wife business team own their own home, a new truck, and are building a 20,000 square-foot facility to house their thriving print-art business, WeSellArt.com. But the couple wasn't always debt free. "In October of 1997, we were laid off from manufacturing plant jobs. We had four kids at the time and were thousands of dollars in debt," said Mike Baker. "I sold knickknacks and memorabilia on eBay. With no job prospects in sight, I stepped up my online sales hobby. I scoured garage sales and auctions. Working from 5:00 A.M. until midnight off of an old, dingy computer, I wrote ads, answered e-mails, wrote out labels, and packed and shipped items. Our reputation as trinket collectors drew calls from locals and auctioneers, including a poster collector who sold us our lucky break. This guy had over 2,000 posters to sell. I gave him $100 for them all and one poster alone fetched $100. Following that, I negotiated contracts with four major manufacturers of high-quality prints and incorporated in 1999." Today, the business has customers from as far away as Kuwait. "I still answer 500 e-mails a day and I'm here from 6:00 A.M. to 8:00 P.M.," said Mike. "But I love it."

When doing business online, don't think local—go global. Multicurrency is the next big thing and will allow transactions from anywhere worldwide.

But beware of online crime. Vendors with resaleable items such as jewelry are highly targeted by fraudsters. Be reputable. E-buyers post feedback about their shopping experience to every seller. Stay honest, prompt, and reliable to win the trust and dollars of customers.

For Richer, For Poorer

You vowed to stick together "in sickness and in health," but how about when one of you gets the corporate ax or takes a major pay cut in order to pursue more fulfilling work? Money woes and lay-offs bring out the worst in us and in our relationships, according to Henry Paul, M.D., a Manhattan-based psychiatrist and author. "Our net worth is directly tied to our self worth. As it drops, people get humiliated by having to ask others for money or to receive public assistance. Self-loathing increases and this hate is often taken out on a spouse or those closest to us," he said.

Since the majority of American households depend on two incomes today, couples should plan for unexpected financial emergencies. "Unfortunately, too many couples don't address money issues before they marry," said Anthony Rabasca, a marriage and family therapist from Rome, New York.

When finances are a root cause of a depressed marriage or relationship, common signs include mounting debt, depression, or one partner becoming self-absorbed, according to the marital expert. Conversely, if one person loses his or her job, but the mate continues to excel in his or her career, competition and resentment often set in. "Men are most vulnerable when they're unemployed. Issues of emotional weakness are highlighted and can lead to a power struggle," Mr. Rabasca added.

Fortunately, for couples willing to acknowledge the problem, there can be a silver lining. "I'd recommend seeking professional help—a third party who can help you sort out what's really important," said Mr. Rabasca.

If your lifestyle has suddenly been threatened due to the economy or job market, Jolie Solomon, deputy editor of *Working Mother* magazine, suggests you get creative.

"If your partner's job provides benefits, the other partner can take on contract work or work from home," she said.

It's also important to retain your dignity. Don't be ashamed. If you've recently lost your job, know that you're not alone. Make peace with any tradeoffs you're making and realize that you may have to keep switching gears—that's just how working life is today.

Know where your money is going. Check your bills for erroneous charges. Reevaluate your approach to spending. Be honest with yourself. If you need debt counseling, get it.

Stay cool for your kids, too. "They pick up on parental anxieties," said Ms. Solomon. "Let them ask questions, but keep things positive. Children need a sense of security."

When joblessness threatens the ties that bind, remember, "There is a grieving process, a sense of loss one experiences when losing a job, which needs to be validated by your partner," said Mr. Rabasca. "It's an opportunity for this person to be there for you when you're struggling with a difficult situation."

Unemployment is a temporary circumstance, Dr. Paul agreed. "Your spouse or partner can help by organizing an employment search and making contacts for you so that you don't feel alone," he said.

When Work Is a Family Affair

What if your soul mate wants to go into business with you? How do you know if you have what it takes to maintain a solid emotional and business alliance? While new business partnerships are formed every day, it takes caution, clear objectives, and complimentary skill sets for such relationships to prosper and last.

John and Susan Maloney say they knew they had the right foundation for going into business together. They had been married for ten years when they decided to start Urbanbaby.com. After years in the fashion and publishing industries, Susan tapped into a niche market on the Internet. "I was pregnant and realized that none of the parenting Web sites offered localized information," she said.

Mr. Maloney, a New Media executive, shared Susan's passion for the idea and recognized the potential business opportunity.

Following months of extensive research and working odd hours and weekends to test market their idea, the twosome left their full-time jobs to launch Urbanbaby.com, an online information and shopping resource, in August of 1999. Their growing network of Web sites targets new and expectant parents who reside in top metropolitan communities.

Throughout their first year in business, the Maloneys have learned much about each other and working together. "It's made me a better communicator," said John. For example, when disagreements arise, the two trade e-mails to identify and resolve issues quickly.

Having a clear division of responsibilities has been integral to their success. As editor in chief, Susan manages the content, services, and production of their sites and online store. Serving as president, John develops strategic alliances with partners and advertisers.

For those thinking of starting up a business with your significant other, "You need to treat each other as professionals and separate the personal aspect," said John. "Figure out what your unique disciplines are and where you overlap."

It takes thoughtful planning to create a productive, fun, and profitable life and business partnership.

Before you take this plunge, consider your history of working together. For example, have you renovated or designed a room in your home or planned your own wedding or special event from start to finish? Such nonbusiness-related projects are good indicators of how well you may fare in the world of business.

Understand that your partner may have different work habits

than you do. If your mate is accustomed to playing music while he types, can you respect your not-so-silent partner?

Living the Dream

Ken and Daria Dolan, talk-show hosts

Each week, when money matters get messy, over 2.5 million Americans, ages twelve and up, turn to *The Dolans*. Married thirty years, husband and wife team Ken and Daria Dolan cohost the popular, personal finance radio call-in show. Before their hit show went on air, the Dolans earned their financial expert hats working in the field. Ken worked as a stockbroker for Boston- and Wall Street–based firms and eventually as vice chairman of an investment bank in Manhattan. Once married to Ken, Daria stayed at home to parent their only daughter, Meredith. She'd never taken a business course, but when Ken announced he was quitting his six-figure job to work in radio, she decided to become a stockbroker to compensate for their shortfall of income. The following year, the Dolans brainstormed the idea of teaming up together on air. Today, *The Dolans* is one of the top ten most listened to radio shows in America, according to *Talkers Magazine*. Understandably, living and working with a spouse isn't always a breeze, admits Daria. "We have gone on the air mad at each other. We may have a verbal fistfight during a commercial break, but we don't think about it when the microphone goes back on," she said. "We keep work and home separate."

Will spending a lot of time together on the job affect your intimacy level and personal relationship or affect the time you have to spend with your children? You'll need to carefully weigh the cost/benefits of this proposition.

Can you take off your business hat? It's unhealthy to let such affairs consume you before, during, and after work hours. If you operate out of a home office all day, perhaps frequent lunches or dinners out are in order. Maybe you can agree to end all business conversation after 5:00 P.M.—particularly if you have kids who will bemoan it.

Hope for the best, but plan for the worst. If things aren't working out, don't let tension fester. Discuss beforehand how you'll handle matters if one of you wants to call it quits.

Summary

Following a career while staying at home, especially if you are the one responsible for the lion's share of the homemaking, has its own stress and difficulties. Making sure that your work and home life don't blur too much is a big part of the equation in making this work.

Tips to remember:

- There are certain jobs that coexist very well as work-from-home endeavors—some even involve using your home as part of the moneymaking enterprise, such as bed and breakfasts. Look into all the angles and legalities before making the decision.
- Set up a home office, even if it's just a corner somewhere. Clearing the dining room table periodically doesn't work. You need a space that's dedicated to your needs.
- You may also have to work at keeping family relationships together and whole, especially if your work or study claims you for long hours. Make sure you keep your work/life balance. Just because you are working at home, doesn't mean you should feel that you never have a time or a place to relax.

Chapter 7

Moving on Up:
Learning to Sell Anything—
Including Yourself

Who doesn't want to be a success story? The good news is you don't have to be the most talented, gorgeous, or ingenious person to win over or influence people. However, there's no quickie formula for creating a lasting product or brand. It takes plenty of sweat equity, marketing, and advertising to inform your customers about who you are and what you're selling, to open doors, create relationships, and close deals.

"There's no such thing as a born salesman," said Stephan Schiffman, founder of DEI Management Group, Inc., a nationally recognized sales training company. "Just because you're not shy and you're a great conversationalist who can shake hands easily doesn't mean you are automatically a good salesperson. Everyone needs to learn certain sales skills. We are always selling, all the time—our concepts, ourselves, our ideas. It's a question of understanding the sales process and making sure you hit the mark." Whether it's a loan or new business prospect you're trying to nab, there are some ways Schiffman suggests you can fine-tune your professional pitch:

- *Do some soul searching.* No one else can motivate you. Find something within that fills you with anticipation for each new day. If you're not excited about your product/talent/service, no one else will be either.

- *Prospect regularly.* Are you networking for new clients or vendors for your product? Are you taking every audition you can get? Are you sending out resumes? A dry spell is the result of months of slacking off, not a sudden downturn. Every day, try to make something happen before lunch. Don't be shortsighted. Think of what you can do for your business today that will have an effect a year from now.

- *When you're about to close a deal, don't blow it.* Assume you're already there, and you will be. Don't question or doubt yourself. Maintain the momentum and presume you'll get the sale.

- *Call clients who have come to you before.* Tell them about what's happening with your business that may trigger a new sale. Did you get a write-up in a local paper? Are you offering new products or services? Even if someone isn't interested, he or she may hook you up with someone who is.

- *First impressions count.* Make sure you're on time, look sharp, and have extra copies of your business proposal, demo tapes, slides, and a list of references.

Marketing your talent/product/service can be scary if you're not used to it. However, the most important thing to remember is that sales is a learned skill. If you're not comfortable with your pitch, then have a trusted friend, mentor, or colleague critique you. Believe in yourself and the value of what you have to offer.

Patently Better

Throughout time, it has been the contributions of artists, inventors, and entrepreneurs that have advanced society. Great innovators, such as Thomas Edison (electric light, phonographs), Alexander Graham Bell (telephone), George Eastman (film), and John Logie Baird (television), developed inventions that have forever improved the way the world lives and works. Inventors seek to make the impossible possible.

However, it takes more than a bright idea and great salesmanship to create a revolutionary product. Whether you're a writer, an artist, or an inventor, you must (legally) protect what you create. Remember that the creative path often intersects the four-square reality of the business world. If you have an invention that you think is marketable, get your idea patented *before* selling it to an existing manufacturer or marketing it for yourself. Your ideas are known as "intellectual property," and if you want them to remain under your control, you need to protect them. Owning a patent gives you the right to stop someone else from making, using, or selling your invention without your permission. However, be aware that getting a patent is no small feat. Navigating your way through the bureaucracy of the U.S. patenting system can be a daunting task. "The day a patent hits the patent office, it can take up to a year before an examiner looks at it," explained Dr. Jon C. Garito, president of Ellman International, Inc., a privately held, leading medical device designer, manufacturer, and marketer based in Hewlett, New York. "The officer may read through a variety of patents that share similar designs to yours. If that is the case you'll have to argue that your product is distinct in size, structure, operation, and intended result," he said.

Patent attorneys can help with the process, but if you can't afford one, you can still conduct a patent search online. If you have Internet access, you can use two Web sites to perform a search. The first site is *www.uspto.gov.* This site is sponsored by the U.S. Patent and Trademark Office (PTO) and allows you to search existing patents. The second site is *www.patents.ibm.com,* which is maintained by IBM and is more comprehensive. It allows you to do more sophisticated searches and displays drawings of the patented products.

Currently, there are drawbacks to this method. "A lot of earlier pat-ent history hasn't been entered yet, so you don't get the full picture using this method," advised Dr. Garito.

In the end, it's not always the fame or fortune that drives many inventors. It's the ability to solve problems and advance civilization. "It's exciting to see your invention put to use," said Alan G. Ellman, the firm's CEO. "We interrelate with physicians, dentists, and vet-erinarians who face surgical obstacles every day. . . . Being able to develop tools for them so that their patients can benefit is a wonder-ful thing—it's what drives me. When we get patients who write us letters, it validates what we're doing," added Dr. Garito.

Get Your Market Share

If you have a one-of-a-kind product that is relatively inexpensive to manufacture yourself, then trade shows, bazaars, and fairs are sen-sible distribution outlets. However, you first want to find out how much everything costs so you can decide how much profit you need to make it worthwhile. You'll need to recoup enough to justify the upfront and hidden costs of establishing your presence. Booth rental and/or set-up fees, travel, food, lodging, printing of marketing col-lateral, employee wages, and promotional items are a few of the key expenses you should be prepared to cover at these events.

Select the shows that are optimal for your particular product and industry and have high levels of visitor traffic. You should be able to find attendance numbers at the event Web site or by contact-ing the event coordinator. It's best to build up your confidence and client base at local shows before working your way up to statewide and national events.

Before you book a booth, it's wise to pay a visit to similar trade shows and talk with other vendors about what kinds of products sell well and how much merchandise you can expect to sell. To keep your costs down, produce a small quantity of your product. When you've secured your own booth, the first step is to create a "wow factor."

For example, you may want to offer a two-for-one special, promotional giveaways, or product raffle.

Living the Dream

Jennifer O'Meara, digital print artist

New artists can be naïve about the business side of the art world. This can be both a blessing and a curse, according to Bill O'Meara, who handles marketing and collections for his acclaimed wife, artist Jennifer O'Meara. "Jennifer and I started our business of selling her digital prints of barns and flowers back in 1992. We used all of our resources to finance the purchase of a specialized, $150,000 printer. It was worth more than our house! I quit my job and started selling Jennifer's artwork full-time. I visited high-end art galleries from SoHo to Santa Fe and within a year had Jennifer's work showing in nearly twenty of them. But galleries take your artwork on consignment and do not pay you for months or sometimes years after they sell it. So over time we started our own gallery in Denver, Colorado, which we ran for about six years. The gallery paid for itself, but we were having much more success selling directly to collectors through fine art festivals and trade shows. During the late 1990s, Jennifer was selling well over $300,000 in artwork a year. Jennifer plans on working with galleries again, but only two or three of the very best and respected galleries, as she knows that good salesmanship involves knowing where to invest your time.

Location is king. Front and center isn't necessarily ideal if it's cramped or crowded together with other booths. You want enough room for a crowd of at least ten to gather.

Announce yourself—and work it! Products don't magically sell themselves like hotcakes. Before you exhibit, attend a couple of shows to watch the styles and methods vendors use to attract customers. If you're not a born salesman, hire someone who can excite and lure patrons. You'll want to keep the buzz going after the show. Word of mouth is the best—and cheapest—form of advertising. Have plenty of leaflets, brochures, and business cards on hand that people can take with them to spread the news of your goods. After the show, analyze what did and didn't work and why. If you weren't a hit, fine-tune your presentation accordingly for the next fair.

Many artists work for the fun of it and just want to be involved in their creative process. They lack financial success because they don't want to take the time to market their products. Realize, you may get burned, maybe even more than once, as you persevere in the business world. There will be plenty of mistakes and setbacks. But after a few successes, you'll have more money, knowledge, and experience, so your business will flourish artistically as well as economically. If your creativity is truly who you are as a person, you have to set it free and let it take you wherever it takes you or forever regret what you have done with your special gift.

Catalog Your Worth

Selling your wares via a catalog might be a good option. Approximately 14.9 billion catalogs are published in the United States each year, generating $120 billion in annual sales, according to Lee Jay Lorenzen, president and CEO of CatalogCity.com, an online catalog super site, which sells a range of products from top-brand catalogs. To have a catalog of your own, you'll need to photograph your goods, design and print the catalog, and then mail and distribute it, often by buying a mailing list or using addresses of your existing client base. You can also set up a Web site instead of, or alongside, the print version.

"Just like the 1-800 number, the Internet is a new channel through which catalog companies can serve customers," said Mr.

Lorenzen, who started his Internet venture with the vision of "Being able to offer consumers convenient, timely, and environmentally friendly access to the world's best products."

If you decide to market your products through a catalog, keep in mind that catalog shoppers are a unique breed. They are often busy people who prefer to save their spare time for fun and leisure, not shopping. Convenience and selection are the keys to winning their trust and loyalty. "Remote shoppers can't touch, taste, or feel your products," said Mr. Lorenzen. "Your job is to deliver a compelling shopping experience and try to convince a person to buy your products at a distance."

With the industry in its infancy, the toughest challenge that online catalog merchants face is providing impeccable customer service. "Consumers should have 'real time' access to a catalog's inventory system to find out whether or not a product is in stock and have the ability to track the shipping and delivery status of their orders." The best way to find out about great customer service is to shop from sites that have high customer satisfaction and emulate what they do. You may want to buy a few products, return them, and make note of the positive aspects of the experience.

Even the smallest entrepreneur can set up a basic shopping site, according to Lorenzen.

"I would view the Web as the ultimate virtual catalog where anyone can test market their product, establish its price, and potential demand," he said. The simplest of all these steps is to start out on eBay and create an auction for your product with a zero reserve price. The ultimate number of bidders and price paid is an indicator of what the demand is and what the price should be. However, be aware that eBay buyers are bargain hunters and are used to buying used products. So, the actual retail price is probably three to five times the typical winning bid. Hopefully, this provides enough margin for your distribution partner.

The next step after eBay auctions would be a stand-alone store on Yahoo or Shop.com. These stores cost a small amount per month plus a commission on the sales. You can then test the effectiveness of traffic generation (attracting customers through online advertising) and marketing on major Internet search engines, and that can tell you how many hits (viewers) you are getting.

Living the Dream

Jules and Allen Allen, owners, Allen Allen

For Allen Allen, a popular women's clothing catalog based in Los Angeles, every page of their quarterly print booklet is designed so that customers feel the personal energy of those behind the business, according to Martin Carpino, their director of operations. Founded in 1986 by husband and wife team Jules and Allen Allen, the business started as one small kiosk, which featured Ms. Allen's self-designed T-shirts. While they never had trouble selling the merchandise, "Financing was difficult," said Mr. Carpino. "We'd have orders, but needed to pay bills in order to get the goods to fulfill them," he admitted. After taking out a bank loan, the Allens constructed a black-and-white catalog, bought mailing lists of potential customers, and eventually contracted out the manufacturing of their label to include a wider variety of garments and fabric types. Today their full-color catalogue boasts a customer database of more than 600,000, with a 20 percent growth rate every year. The once small operation has added its own fulfillment center, customer service department, and design showrooms across the country. An online catalogue is in the creative stage.

After making the business work on a small, online-only scale, the next step might be to place a small single product ad in carefully chosen magazines. Again, measure the response the ad generates—if any. Does it generate good PR, drive people to your Web site, and most importantly, create sales? The data from your efforts will help you decide whether you should continue to operate in this mode or partner with an existing cataloger or other channel of distribution. Leaders in the industry understand that beyond their product offerings, it's a lifestyle and frame of mind they're selling.

Many folks compare the relatively new field of Internet marketing to the much older and established field of direct-mail marketing and, specifically, niche catalog selling through the good old postal service. Yet, we all have our specialized tastes and interests. Niche catalogs that address such needs are thriving today. There are a lot of questions to ask yourself before diving into this type of business— are you ready to finance the inventory you publish in your catalog? Do you have the facilities for warehousing and shipping your products? How will you distribute your catalog? If so, how much are the printing costs? For help on how to launch a successful catalog business, check out books on the subject such as *Creating a Profitable Catalog: Everything You Need to Know to Create a Catalog That Sells* by Jack Schmid (McGraw-Hill/Contemporary Books).

Perfect Pitch

You don't need to hire a public relations firm on a costly retainer to create a buzz about your product or service. In fact, an expensive promotional budget can kill your small business. There are plenty of free, or dirt-cheap, outlets for shameless promotion right at your fingertips, according to George Mackenzie, a veteran television anchor and radio talk show host and publisher of the "Publicity Goldmine" e-zine. To land affordable publicity, you need to create a win-win relationship between yourself and the media you are pitching to. To accomplish that, here are some rules that you should follow:

1. *Don't come across as an overly aggressive, publicity monger.* Media professionals have jobs to do just like anyone

else, so create a mutually beneficial association. The easier you can make their job and the better you can help to serve their audience, the more likely you are to get a positive publicity result.

2. *Timing is everything.* Reporters are always on the prowl for news items that tie in to holidays or national news and events. If you can relate or localize your story idea to accommodate these needs, you may get yourself some column inches.

3. *Use your hometown media.* The local press regularly features local business owners who are contributing to the area economy. Submit a press release about your venture to the regional newspapers, television, and radio stations. Come up with a catchy hook or angle to peak their interest in profiling your business.

4. *Call the new kid on the block.* If a reporter is new to his job, you can bet he's on the hunt for stories that will impress his boss. Target these raw recruits. Position yourself as a great resource, someone who can be relied upon for a helpful quote.

5. *Build a media database.* Keep track of the valuable media contacts you're building. Update their information regularly as these folks tend to move around.

6. *Spread the word in cyberspace.* You can tap a huge source of potential customers through e-mail marketing. Research electronic magazines and newsletter publishers that focus on stories/content related to your business. Such outlets target thousands of potential customers who have opted to regularly receive the latest information on that subject.

The most important thing to remember about marketing and selling your product or talent is to target your pitch. Instead of blanketing the country with news faxes, be selective about your publicity targets. Choose industry and trade publications that fit your venture, and try to find beat reporters who regularly cover topics of relevance to your product or service. For example, lifestyle magazines often have designated writers who cover new products, antiques and collectibles, or food and entertaining. And most city newspapers have a small business section. Find out the name of the person you need to address and then send your press release or media kit directly to these writers. Sending material without names and titles will mean your package ends up in the big pile of unopened envelopes in the mailroom. Follow up to ascertain their interest in covering your story.

Sum it up in a sound bite. Narrow your pitch to one or two sentences that arouse curiosity. Television news anchors are great at teasing an audience before a commercial break. Observe them in action for style and content ideas.

If you feel you know your industry inside out, become an authority on the subject. Try penning a column about industry trends, marketing strategies, or new products for leading trade magazines—or even local ones. Also, radio and television producers routinely seek out guest experts for their programming. To prepare for such segments (typically ten to twenty minutes long), send producers a list of questions to ask you in advance. This allows you to prepare before the interview and enables you to come across as intelligent as possible.

Lastly, be ready for your close-up and take advantage of the media coverage you receive. If you can't deliver the goods and services you've promised, you'll drive customers away.

There's Work in the Word "Network"

Is tonight your laundry night? Do you have to baby-sit your neighbor's sick cat? If you've run out of excuses for blowing off another networking event, it's time to face the crowd. Entrepreneurs in particular can't afford to miss out on such opportunities. To expand your business you need to invest in face time with people. Even the best marketing materials don't have the same impact as connecting with people and selling them your product, service, or talent.

The first step toward savvy schmoozing comes from identifying and removing the roadblock that intimidates you. For most people, it's the unwillingness to risk rejection. Most people feel it's better to be safe than sorry. But this attitude prevents you from developing effective communication skills and puts you at risk for missing out on business, career, and social opportunities.

There's no doubt that in today's competitive business climate, being pleasantly pushy is an asset, perhaps even necessary in beating your competition and getting ahead. But there is a fine line between being effective and being overly aggressive. You need to know how to handle yourself properly at networking opportunities.

Relationship building is still the key to opening doors for yourself in your work life. Andrea Nierenberg, president of The Nierenberg Group, a consulting firm that specializes in management training, suggests you practice a self-introduction. Give your name, who and what you represent, and what your commonality is with those at the event. Carry a healthy supply of business cards. You don't want to run out just before an important introduction. Always replenish your wallet after an event.

See the potential in every person you meet. Too often we shoot for the top person in charge, without realizing that the strength is in the foundation. Don't discount someone as unimportant. Get to know a decision maker's receptionist or assistant. Take care of these people—they have the boss's ear a lot more than you do.

Listen with sincerity. Curiosity in other people goes a long way at an event. Be interested in the people you are mixing with. People love to talk about themselves. Don't just hear what someone is saying. Focus intently on this person. If you find yourself talking more than 50 percent in a conversation, you're talking too much.

Also, don't show up at an industry networking event just once; come to meetings regularly. If you attend infrequently or neglect to learn anything about the organization or your audience, people will see you as a taker. Good networking is about giving as much as receiving. Before arriving, read the association newsletter to find out what the theme of the session is and who's speaking. Plan to target a few people there. Not every lead will turn into a great thing. It's a process.

Determine the best way to keep in touch with contacts. Find out how new business contacts prefer to communicate. Learn whether someone prefers to respond by voice or e-mail. After you know how people want to be contacted, follow up in unique ways. Take mental notes of a person's hobbies or interests, which can springboard future communications. It's a tremendous relationship builder when you can recall something that's important to someone. It just takes a little thought and attention to detail.

Also, never forget to say thank you. There's nothing worse than when you put a friend in touch with a colleague or associate, and that friend neglects to update you or acknowledge the link you made. You must thank people right down the line. Even if nothing comes out of a connection, be gracious and keep sources in the loop. If you've received the benefit of wisdom, advice, or support from someone at an event, acknowledge it. Following up with a thank-you note, on paper in your own writing, speaks volumes.

Ask and You Shall Receive

What do some people dread more than a root canal? Negotiating! Whether it's asking for a raise, shopping for a car, or any other situation that requires bargaining for their own interests, most people dread the thought of negotiating. Beyond landing a job or promoting your side business, a knack for selling yourself and being able to communicate persuasively helps you close deals, secure promotions, win projects, and even receive help with housework.

"Start incorporating [deal making] into your everyday life," advises Linda Babcock, professor of economics at Carnegie Mellon University's H. John Heinz School of Public Policy and Management.

The key to effective persuasion is to ask for what you want. Don't worry about being perceived as pushy or aggressive. Working hard and doing a good job in itself won't guarantee a promotion or audition. Don't back down at the first sign of resistance. It's not the end of the world to get a no. Other strategies to keep in mind include:

- *Choose admirable mentors.* It's important to be mentored by people in positions of power in your organization or artistic circle. They are critical assets in one's professional life. When choosing a mentor, select someone who is good at something you admire or wish to improve upon.
- *Strive for a win-win situation.* Instead of a competitive approach, take a collaborative one. Find out what's important to your negotiating partner. There's something that both sides want, otherwise you wouldn't be at the table. This is the key to reaching better agreements.
- *Overprepare.* Practice your pitch with a friend. Notice your body language. What you radiate bears directly on the responses you will command from colleagues. Gestures can spell out frustration, defensiveness, or openness. Do you laugh nervously? Do you converse while gazing eye to eye? To project confidence, control your tone of voice, speed of delivery, and volume.

The most important component of a negotiation is information. Educate yourself and be informed. For instance, if you're asking for more money, know that the extra you're asking for is reasonable. Visit *www.salary.com* to assess whether your experience warrants increased pay. Investigate what your work is worth in the marketplace. Consult industry publications and Web sites, and use your social and professional networks to find out an appropriate price to charge (it's OK to ask others what they charge!). Don't low-ball yourself. Creative people in particular often feel uncomfortable asking to be compensated well for work that they love. You need to set a fairly aggressive asking price going into negotiation and overcome the urge to accept a small payment. In fact, if you *never* get claims that your rate is too high, it means you probably aren't charging enough! Just because you love what you do doesn't mean you can't make a lot of money doing it.

Those Who Can, Teach

Another way to instantly boost your net worth, promote your product or service, and earn extra income is by becoming an "expert" in your field. Just skim the courses offered through your local college or university's continuing education program. You're certain to find a line-up of skilled watercolorists, tax wizards, and novelists who moonlight as instructors while holding down day jobs just like yourself.

You don't need a Ph.D. to teach most subjects, but you do need passion for your subject and plenty of real-world experience. This means that if you're a screenwriter who wants to teach others how to pen their first movie, you'll need the credentials to back it up, including prior experience as a working writer. To pitch a course, most universities require you to submit your resume and a written curriculum and to prepare an in-person presentation.

Aside from earning extra income ($30 per hour and up) for an up-and-coming proprietor, those teaching appearances can help to raise your business profile within the community.

Before you try to instruct students, realize that just because you're well versed in a subject doesn't mean you are able to teach it. You need to be a good communicator and highly organized. A lot of people have the knowledge but can't convey it to someone else. Fortunately, some schools offer personalized teacher training programs and materials.

Hot subjects on the teaching circuit now include crafts such as quilting, photography, and knitting as well as computer courses, entrepreneurship, pharmacy, nursing and paralegal careers, childcare, and time management.

Living the Dream

Joseph Abboud, founder and chief creative director, Joseph Abboud Company

Joseph Abboud is on the short list of designers who have "arrived," and he has no intention of disappearing off the fashion map anytime soon. After college graduation, he took advantage of a scholarship to La Sorbonne in Paris, where he soaked up the fashion scene. When he returned to America, Abboud took a sales position at Ralph Lauren, and within three years rose to become the associate director of design for the company's men's line. However, Abboud still felt he had more to offer the market. Operating out of a tiny Manhattan office, Abboud independently financed a small menswear collection. It was a huge success, and his signature style was well received by major specialty stores such as Bergdorf Goodman and Neiman Marcus. Today, Abboud's men's collections are available in select stores throughout the United States, Canada, and Asia. In his fifties, Abboud has proudly remained true to his design identity, without having to succumb to the fashion media. "Everything evolves," he said. "But good designers stay true to concept."

Summary

Dealing with the business end of things often feels like drudgery for creative types, but it's essential for success. Don't be afraid of it.

Tips to remember:

- Selling yourself is the first step to selling your product.
- Look into different ways you can get the word out.
- Network to get your name known.

Chapter 8

Don't Fade Away:
Avoiding Burnout When Juggling
Your Passion and Your Day Job

Almost everyone is familiar with the adage "All work and no play makes Jack a dull boy" (and Jill a dull girl). However, all work and no play can also lead to physical and emotional exhaustion—otherwise known as burnout.

If you are working a full-time job and pursuing your passion during your "off" hours, it's probably inevitable that you're going to burn the candle at both ends from time to time. Unfortunately, the demands of making a living today often keep us working in the office during lunch hour, using the laptop on our commute home, and occasionally treating our significant others to an apologetic take-out dinner after we've had to work late all week. But it's important to know when to schedule downtime, take a break from your side project, or even call in sick when you're exhausted and burned out.

Workaholics, however, carry on regardless day in, day out. Their batteries are constantly charged. Workaholic red flags include the following: rushing, restlessness, scheduling back-to-back appointments, a resistance to delegate tasks, perfectionism, family neglect, and even slacking off on personal hygiene. This nonstop pace can evoke distressful symptoms such as depression, anxiety, and exhaustion.

Surprisingly, work addiction isn't even caused in the workplace, according to Bryan E. Robinson, psychotherapist and professor of counseling at the University of North Carolina, Charlotte, and author of *Chained to the Desk: A Guidebook for Workaholics, Their Partners and Children, and the Clinicians Who Treat Them* (NYU Press). It has its roots in childhood family dysfunction, as work addicts are often children of alcoholics or workaholic parents, he claims. "Workaholics become dependent on their work/occupation to define who they are and to gain a positive sense of themselves," he added. They dive into their work as an escape or psychological safe haven.

Another enabling force is the advertising industry, which glamorizes work addiction. The message of many of the commercials for cell phones and electronic organizers is that technology, information, and mobility equal power and a ticket into a more elite class.

Unfortunately for the families of work addicts, relationships suffer enormous consequences. In their loneliness, the spouse or mate of a workaholic often experiences a loss of intimacy, powerlessness, and resentment. Adult children of work addicts tend to grow up "self-critical, depression-prone, angry, and unsuccessful in their intimate relationships," writes the author.

Support does exist for those prepared to accept it. Mr. Robinson encourages family members to "express their feelings about their problems, refrain from making alibis for the workaholic family member's absenteeism from social functions, and let their loved one be responsible for explanations."

The attitudes necessary for overcoming this illness begin with the workaholic. They should not resort to the blame game, but neither should they get off easy. Workaholics have to learn to set limits on their work patterns, refrain from unrealistic deadlines, set aside daily personal time, and take work more lightly and play more seriously in order to help restore their work/life balance.

Two decades ago, burnout almost professionally derailed Cindy McIntyre, a registered nurse, wife, and mother of two from

Newtown, Connecticut. Worn out and low on both self-esteem and money, Cindy discovered that in order to heal her essence, she would have to get a grip on her finances. Yes, interestingly enough, fiscal ineptitude is a key reason why women especially often fail to shower themselves with TLC.

"Girls are taught that it's impolite to publicly discuss money matters, like how much a person has in the bank or what kind of car they drive. When they begin working, they don't know how to budget properly or how much discretionary income they actually have," explained Dr. Dorothy Cantor, a practicing psychologist from Westfield, New Jersey.

If you take a closer look at where your hard-earned paycheck disappears to each month, chances are, you'll be less inclined to deny yourself life's little luxuries. Since learning this valuable lesson, Cindy afforded herself the time and money required to earn a bachelor's degree in her field—a longstanding objective. She also splurges on herself once a week, without forking over a small fortune.

Avoiding Creative Burnout

Lost that lovin' feeling for your day job? Feel like you're making a living as opposed to making a life? Realize, there are many stressors that cause career burnout (personal life, physical exhaustion, etc.). For some people, a side project or business may not be the answer. The extra anxiety and challenge may swallow you up. To invite more balance into your life, take an honest inventory of your life and borrow some of these tips:

- *Think back to the last time you learned something new.* It's refreshing to get back to a "beginner's mind," even if it's not industry specific or relevant to your career.
- *It pays to prioritize.* Know which tasks must be accomplished today and which can wait for tomorrow. Ask for help when you need it. Whether you delegate to employees, partner with

other firms or vendors, or simply network for support and advice, share your load. In your personal life, hire baby sitters or housekeeping staff so you can clear your overcrowded schedule, catch up on rest, and make clear-headed decisions about deferring or shedding some of your responsibilities.

- *Hard to keep your pet project secret?* If you lack privacy at work, the need to preserve confidentiality may be another source of stress. Find a trustworthy friend or professional counselor you can confide in.

- *Take off.* Whether for an hour or a month, take a vacation for some much-needed R&R. Do something that gives you maximum pleasure. Pamper yourself as if you had a physical illness. Even a short walk allows you to burn off nervous energy while taking in exercise and the scenery. You'll think more clearly than if you stayed chained to your desk.

- *You are what you eat.* Busy people can be chronic meal skippers or too frequently consume junk food on the go. Instead, refuel with veggies, fruits, and high-energy snacks.

Don't forget to hydrate yourself! Most people don't drink enough water and end up dehydrated, cranky, and tired. Water helps flush out bodily toxins. Try this natural pick-me-up instead of caffeinated sodas or coffee.

It can be hard to maintain perspective when you're burning the candle at both ends. Just remember, the fact that you've got so much going on speaks to how talented and capable you are. The next time you feel scattered or out of control, take a few slow, deep breaths to relax and collect yourself.

Fish or Cut Bait

Do you remember your first flying leap off the diving board? Your first plane ride? The first blind date you agreed to let your mother fix you up on? Life is a series of firsts. Each time we risk what's safe and familiar about our lives and decide instead to bet on ourselves, we take one step closer to true happiness and success.

Living the Dream

Andrea McGinty, founder, It's Just Lunch

"You get to that scary point when you ask yourself, 'Am I ready to jump or not?'" said Andrea McGinty. In 1991, after her own marital engagement was called off, McGinty devised a winning business concept—a specialized dating service that would accommodate busy twenty- to fifty-year-old professionals. While holding down her marketing day job (and income) at a technology firm, she worked on her new venture before and after work hours. When her business was just a month old, McGinty was interviewed on a local classic rock radio station in Chicago to discuss dating issues and promote her new service. To McGinty's horror, her coworkers were among the listening audience, and her cover was blown. "I knew there would be ramifications. To avoid any conflict, I made up my mind to quit my job so I could seize my new opportunity. Once I left, my heart went into my business 120 percent," she said. Today, McGinty has no regrets about her decision. She is rich in both love and work. Her franchise operation has expanded to fifty locations nationwide, she's been happily married for a decade, and her firm posted annual revenues of $24 million for 2003. "There's no bigger high. When I go to weddings or receive holiday cards from couples we've arranged, it feels so good," declared McGinty.

If you are underpaid and unfulfilled in your present occupation, then you may be in danger of burnout even if you aren't clocking sixty-hour weeks. Don't let self-doubt or self-judgment impede your progress. You may be able to sidestep into a career that is closer to your artistic bent. For instance, if you work within the industry you aspire to, you can actively augment your creative dream. Examples are journalists who become authors, public relations pros who are performers, film studio workers who are actors, and advertising execs who are artists.

If you have been leading a double life—holding down your day job while trying to launch a side gig—don't wait until you're tank is running on empty. Analyze your financial situation and determine which direction you can afford to put all of your time and energy into.

Beyond the emotional and physical ramifications, we're apt to be unproductive on the job and less motivated to keep on track with our career goals when our energy reserves are depleted. The time may come when your creative dream necessitates your complete and utter attention. You may be doing a disservice to your day job and your side gig by keeping one hand in each pot. Keep your finances in order so that you're prepared to leave your day job and commit to your new venture if necessary. On the flip side, if mental and bodily exhaustion begin to overtake you, you may need to put your project on hold and put your health first.

Handling Rejection

Burnout can be emotional as well as physical. If your art is a reflection of your heart and soul, hearing the words "Thanks, but I'm afraid we'll pass" can cut like a knife. Many great artists, including van Gogh were never recognized in their lifetime. Getting auditions, casting calls, or financing for a new venture is hard. The day-in, day-out rejection causes many talented people to give up on their dream before they make it. But let's face it. You may be too old to be the next Eminem or too inexperienced a dancer to tour with Britney. Chances are, at some point you will have to handle the negative aspects of reaching for the stars.

Great art is not only subjective, but subjected to the commercial taste of the masses. If you want to receive both recognition and reward for your work, you can't internalize criticism. Developing a thick skin is an essential part of a true artist's survival kit. Learn to take a yes as easily as a no. When one door slams in your face, pick yourself up and find another way in.

Living the Dream

Rob Jones, comic book artist

"I've received 700 rejection letters. After the first one, I thought, 'Now there's someone I have to prove wrong.' I've learned not to take rejection personally and to keep my day job," laughed Rob Jones of Jacksonville, Florida. At age twelve, the talented sketch artist was awestruck by the cartoon world. I'd seen the Batman movie and a friend of mine had a comic book version of it. While he'd been drawing since he could hold a pencil, learning about the comic book profession provided him with a goal. He trained at the ultra competitive Joe Kubert School, where many famous comic artists have taught. After school, Rob quickly discovered how limited his prospects were for making money at his craft. To make ends meet, Rob has worked the night shift at a bowling alley and held jobs in graphic design. He spends his free time honing his technique and submitting his creations to publishers. Recently, Rob got his lucky break when he was hired by a comic book veteran to "ink backgrounds" on a project-by-project basis. Although the job market is tight, Rob has no intention of giving up on his passion. "It's such a creative outlet for me. After a long, stressful day I can come home and still feel productive," he said.

Summary

Trying to do too much leads to achieving very little. Burnout comes from many sources: working too many hours, doing too many different tasks, taking on too many projects, and setting unrealistically high standards. Learn to see the signs of burnout and switch gears before you are totally eaten up.

Tips to remember:

- There are many reasons for burnout, including being under-challenged in your job. Examine what it is that's making you feel so exhausted, and work to change it.

- Another source of stress is rejection, as well as the fear of rejection. Yet rejection is a fact of life, and no one has ever gone his or her whole life without meeting it in some shape or form. The more you put on the line, the more you stand to win—or lose. Don't be afraid of it, learn how to deal with it, and roll with the punches, and you stand a better chance of ultimate success.

Chapter 9

Strategies for Success:
Getting the Job You Want

While most job seekers are evaluated by their credentials, skills, and experience, creative professionals must think out of the box when marketing themselves in order to land work. Rather than selling a tangible product, you are promoting yourself as a brand. Think of it as Corporation YOU. Sometimes, getting your foot in the door may mean breaking the rules and ditching those all-too-common, dead-end, job-seeking strategies.

"Creative professionals can demonstrate some of their creativity and not be judged adversely. The rules are different," agrees Sheree Sayles, principal and director of client service, Sayles Graphic Design, of Des Moines, Iowa. For example, to get noticed, one job applicant sent helium-filled balloons with an attached note that read, "Ready to rise up in the world," said Sayles. She recalled another time when "an illustrator left a life-sized character cut-out he'd drawn on cardboard on the front steps of our firm. The figure had his resume in hand. It was effective and we were impressed," she said.

But realize, there is a fine line between clever and *too* cute. "One prospect sent us a picture of himself, lounging on a beach in sandals, during Spring Break. He assumed that we had a laid-back atmosphere and was trying to tell us he'd fit right in. But if he had researched our firm and observed our client list (Maytag, United Airlines), he would have known how inappropriate that tactic was," said Sayles.

Whether you're a soon-to-be college grad or reentering the workforce after a hiatus, here are some more of Sayles's empowering, job-winning tips for creative types.

1. *Dress to impress.* Don't assume that a funky, creative firm has a casual dress code. Err on the side of caution and dress professionally for interviews.

2. *Avoid information overload.* Unless you're applying to a company that specializes in Internet work, refrain from e-mailing your design portfolio or directing a personnel director to different Web sites that you've designed. Checking out your creations means extra work (including downloads) for hiring managers. Instead, submit hard copies via snail mail.

3. *Remember the bottom line.* Recent college grads often present pretty designs or class project work to prospective ad or design agencies for consideration. However, these examples may not demonstrate your ability to conceptualize or sell a message in the real world. To showcase these skills and your ambition, volunteer to design pieces for different organizations. Many small businesses are strapped for cash and would welcome an offer for free graphic design or marketing support. There are also plenty of nonprofits that could use your artistic talents for marketing collateral.

4. *Let your personality shine.* Your cover letter is the perfect opportunity to let your personality come through to employers. Unlike more traditional employers, creative firms such as ad agencies often look at a cover letter as a work sample—so show off your writing skills and design sensibility. However, make sure your letter speaks to your

experience and qualifications, and pay attention to details such as spelling. Don't assume a creative business will be lax about carelessness.

5. *Interview your interviewer.* Job interviewing is a two-way street. You should evaluate whether or not you'll fit into a firm's culture and how suitable its clients are to your disposition, style, and skills. For example, do you ideally want to work on promotions or campaigns for trade magazines, or would you rather handle funkier accounts such as snowboard companies and record labels?

6. *Research your prospects.* Know something about the company you're applying to. Check out their Web site, corporate literature, and annual report. Prepare to demonstrate your knowledge with insightful questions during the interview. Come prepared. Bring a portfolio of work samples to your interview. Practice your responses to anticipated questions so that your comfort level is high. Remember, your interviewer is trying to glean how good a communicator you are in addition to how well your skills match the position description.

7. *Be pleasantly forthright.* Follow up is important, but do not besiege your interviewer with daily phone calls to find out the status of your employment candidacy. Many creative firms run tight ships and do not have dedicated human resources departments. So be considerate—your interviewer has limited billable hours!

Remember, too, that your approach to winning someone over varies from person to person. Perhaps your interviewer was in a sour mood the day of your interview. If you are passed over for a position, politely find out why. Were you under- or overqualified? Listen to the reply and don't interrupt. Develop different ways to overcome or compensate for every negative perception.

Tactical Maneuvers

While there are rules of etiquette for finding a job, such standards don't always cut it for those in creative professions. In a tight labor market, outlandish job hunting tactics often outweigh ordinary strategies. Below are a few maneuvers that have yielded results.

Dare to be different

"I knew someone who wanted to work for a dessert wine company. He videotaped two well-known chefs using the company's wine products and sent the video advertisement into his target employer to demonstrate his marketing savvy."—Jeffrey Fox, owner of Fox & Co., Inc., a marketing consulting firm based in Avon, Connecticut.

Use the old "bait and catch"

"I have heard tales of people holding a moving sale to pitch people about getting a job."—Marcus Ronaldi, founder, Pink Slip Events

Go the extra mile

"I knew an MBA who missed the scheduled, on-campus recruitment period of a particular consulting firm. He paid for his own ticket to fly to the employer's Chicago headquarters, walked into the office in his best suit, told the receptionist that he was in the area "on business," and asked to speak with the managing director. He managed to speak with a top partner at the firm. Though he wasn't hired on the spot, he did get a job offer within a couple of weeks. Aside from his talents and interviewing skills, he wouldn't have gotten it without the guts and initiative."—Jon Housman, cofounder of Jungle Media Group, publisher of magazines for young business executives, New York, New York

Be classy

"A package or material that's courier-delivered overnight is always more impressive than something sent in the regular mail.

It sends signals of importance, power and demonstrates that you cared enough to send something in a mode even better than first-class!"—Carol A. Poore, director of communication, New West Energy, Phoenix, Arizona

Be thorough

"Along with a sharp cover letter and resume, I've found that if there is a value-added article, work sample, or an additional attachment that showcases the person's knowledge, this can be instructional and help the candidate stand out."—Monica Ramirez, president, Zalia Cosmetics, Inc.

Focus on the details

"I know a senior marketing executive who says she throws out resumes that are printed in Times Roman font, because hers is a creative business and Times Roman is bland and unoriginal."—Jon Housman, cofounder of Jungle Media Group, publisher of magazines for young business executives, New York, New York

Take self-promotion to a new level

"During interviews for jobs over the last couple of years, I started touting my Web site, *www.workingfortheman.com*, a side project of mine that humorously and sometimes derisively depicts the world of work. I felt it was impressive enough to show potential employers. Interviewers were slightly uncomfortable—they didn't know whether to laugh about the site or use it as a check against me. But one time, the interviewer brightened up and said, 'You do that site? I check it out all the time. It's really funny.' And I indeed landed that job."—Jeffrey Yamaguchi, author

Blow your own trumpet

"I once received a 'press kit' from a job candidate. He included his photo, which was professionally done, with a photo caption, his bio (one page), background material on himself, and a press release about his potential appointment at my firm. He also created a logo and put it on the cover and on every page in the press kit. I was impressed and it definitely stood out."—Hilary JM Topper, president HJMT Public Relations, LLC, Long Beach, New York

Let your creativity shine

"I know a woman who was interested in becoming a sales rep for Hershey's Chocolate. She arrived at our job fair with a giant, bowling ball–sized Hershey's Kiss that was handmade from foil. The little strip of paper that appears from the top was her cleverly folded resume. The job fair recruiter was wowed by her creativity and by her clear commitment to going the extra mile. She was invited to interview further with the company and is in line for a position."—Tory Johnson, CEO, Women for Hire

Hiring managers at creative firms are seeking bright, imaginative minds. Therefore, a textbook resume may not suffice. To land the creative job of your dreams, you'll need to think out of the box and perhaps off the wall to get noticed, heard, and hired.

Mind Your Mentors

Aside from your uncle Joe or third-grade music teacher, mentors are those people who selflessly pencil in a bit of their time to positively influence your creative and professional path. The art of mentoring comes in a variety of forms. Common practices include shadowing, coaching, helping to strategize real-life issues and decisions, and providing constructive feedback. Now more than ever, mentors are becoming critical assets in professional life. They may invite you to networking events or client meetings, during which time you increase your visibility, showcase your talents, and gain contacts.

When choosing a mentor, select someone who is good at something you admire and wish to improve, such as negotiating skills, the power to influence others, or the ability to close a deal. Someone who has a personality or style that is very different from your own can strengthen your competence in an area in which you're less capable. Additional criteria to consider when choosing a mentor include their availability, temperament, and life experience.

If you already have a job in your desired field, you may be able to find a mentor in your company or organization. If you are in a creative field or have yet to land your dream job, there are other avenues you can pursue. Most industries such as advertising, public relations, and graphic design have professional associations that you can join for an annual fee. These organizations are set up to foster networking and mentoring. If you're a recent graduate, check with a professor or alumni association about finding someone to connect with in your desired field. Also, don't forget the value of peer mentors. Ask someone in your acting class, your writing group, or a fellow intern out to coffee. They may have valuable contacts and insights to offer.

Remember that mentors are busy people. It's important to define your needs, be organized, and approach your mentor with a specific request. It's also important to let your mentor know that he or she is a positive influence in your life. Sending e-mails, voice mails, or written notes, which share examples of your progress and express your appreciation, are surefire ways to reinforce the positive impact your mentor is making in your life. Appreciation and feedback will fuel their interest in investing more time in your development.

Fair Comments

Why do some people sweat at the thought of attending a job fair, while others get revved up to go? It depends on how you perceive the experience. If you view the event as a limited time to promote yourself within a competitive, crowded atmosphere, then it can indeed seem overwhelming. But if you're well prepared, your objectives are clear, and you use the occasion to further your career goals, your time may be well worth the investment.

There are a host of career fair events throughout the year. Today's job expositions are becoming more industry-based and specific to the level of candidates they seek to attract.

Admission is typically free for job seekers. And with some companies paying as much as $5,000 per booth, you can bet they're in a hiring mood.

If you're just starting out in the workforce, job fairs are goldmines for expanding your contacts and testing a variety of corporate waters before diving in. Preparation is key to maximizing your time at any job fair. A confident attitude scores points, so practicing your self-introduction may be helpful. Your greeting should include your name and a tag line, which gives employers a reason to remember you. A bit of humor never hurts. Speak clearly, look people in the eye, and make sure your handshake is firm. A limp grasp may give a weak impression.

Bring enough resumes (at least thirty), and, as you distribute them to hiring personnel, make sure they reciprocate with their business cards. A job fair isn't a resume drop; it's an information exchange. If nametags are distributed, wear one. That way the recruiter will be able to address the potential recruit (you) by name, which is preferable. Dress in appropriate business attire and wear comfortable shoes. You won't be at your peak if your high heels are causing blisters.

Research the backgrounds of any "hot firms" you're interested in meeting with ahead of time. You'll demonstrate your interest, converse more intelligently, and impress hiring managers. If you have your heart set on a particular firm, ask about the types of career possibilities that exist company-wide. There may be a lot more than meets the eye. This is your time to size up the firm and determine whether or not you should invest any more time in pursuing opportunities there. Close your meeting with the recruiter by expressing your interest, qualifications, and availability for an on-site interview. Inquire about the amount of time it typically takes for the firm to respond to resume submissions.

After the fair, your follow-up etiquette can make or break a recruiter's interest in you. Always write a note thanking a hiring representative for speaking with you. It distinguishes you from other candidates and reiterates your serious interest in a company.

Work for Peanuts

The search for talented employees is fierce. For many employers, good grades and the right college major aren't enough. Today's top firms seek employees who are ambitious and who have paid their dues in the working world, even for entry-level posts.

If there are no job slots available at your employer of choice, you might offer to work an internship for a stipulated time period. After you've proven yourself and your capabilities, ask the company to reconsider you for a paid position.

About 80 percent of all college seniors nationwide participated in at least one internship before graduation in 2000, according to Mark Oldman, cofounder of Vault.com, an online, industry-targeted career community. "And that number will continue to grow higher," he said. "The days of internship experience being a luxury are gone. A recent college graduate will be at a competitive disadvantage without it." Organizations are increasingly turning to their own interns to find permanent workers. "Employers are viewing their internship programs as cost-effective bullpens to test out potential employees, before offering them a job," said Oldman.

For students, internships offer a window seat to every aspect of their chosen career field. As temporary observers within a hierarchical setting, it's a time to be a professional sponge and soak up as much knowledge as possible. Superstar interns are typically adept at following through and possess a good attitude and a willingness to go above and beyond their basic duties, according to Warren Wartell, associate director of the faculty student association at SUNY Stony Brook of Long Island, New York. "You need to build up the confidence to take on more responsibility. A certain percentage of your time should be spent on building soft skills such as negotiating, writing, and listening," he said.

Although the word "intern" has sometimes been viewed as someone low on the corporate totem pole, in today's workforce, internships are typically paid (except when a student is to receive academic credit for the experience). Depending on a student's skills and related experience, a company may pay a student a salary or a lump, weekly stipend commensurate with his or her abilities. Some companies even cover housing costs, travel expenses, and such perks as brown bag luncheons with executives and outings to sporting events. While there are still students willing to work for free or next-to-nothing, many companies are adding incentives like flexible hours, networking opportunities, and performance bonuses.

Ten Tips for a Successful Internship Program

1. Be sure you're assigned a mentor or someone on staff who can periodically check on how you're progressing and adapting.
2. Introduce yourself around your firm. An official greeting will include you as part of the team.
3. Have a realistic outlook about your potential tasks. Some industry segments, such as public relations, entail plenty of phone work and faxing. The more menial work should be discussed upfront. Ask plenty of questions to best define the tasks at hand.
4. Familiarize yourself with company rules and policies. The staff may feel right at home, but you are new to their protocols.
5. Expose yourself to other departments of interest. You should seek a well-rounded learning experience. Organize appointments with staff ahead of time to ensure their availability.
6. Schedule regular check-in conversations with your mentor. Such feedback sessions help track progress and problems and open up issues for discussion.

7. Sit in during general meetings of company-wide concern. Such gatherings demonstrate the importance of brainstorming, voicing opinions, and settling differences.
8. Accompany a coworker to an industry networking event. Contact building is an important professional skill to develop early in your career.
9. Complete a final project. You should leave the experience with something to show for it.
10. Ask colleagues and supervisors to serve as references for your job search. Be sure to ask for a letter of recommendation for your file.

By approaching your internship strategically, you can parlay a few months or even a semester's worth of employment into lifelong skills and contacts that can jumpstart your career.

Going It Alone

Depending on your field, freelancing can be a great career path. You are in charge of your own success. You can work on the projects you want, work with a variety of clients, and set your own rates and hours—without being reined in by a boss or company policy. While freelancing has its perks—freedom, no office politics—don't expect it to be easier than a staff job. It's just different, with bigger opportunities for winning and losing. Those who choose this work style must be prepared for the slack that can come with it, wavering income levels, and zero health or retirement benefits.

To freelance successfully, most of your time should be spent on searching out new clients. "It's an ongoing task. The thought should be constant, and you shouldn't think of it as separate from your freelance activities," recommends George Sorensen, Marketing Communications Manager for MC Gill Corp., and the author of *Power Freelancing* (Mid-List Press).

You don't need to be overly aggressive to succeed at freelancing, but you do need to be assertive and create your own momentum. So if you're introverted, you'll need to build up your salesmanship skills or take a class on the subject, since you're sure to hit dry spells in between projects. "Try to put at least an hour a day into prospecting," said Sorensen. "Do as much as you can without burning out, and stay happy about it.

When business is slow, cut your overheads and find a supplemental income area.

Try not to go into debt. It can cripple your abilities to promote when the market gets better. Learn to budget and save, put money aside." Marilyn Howard, founder of Creative Freelancers Inc., on the Web at *www.freelancers.com*, added, "A slow market is not your fault. You'll need to be able to take rejection and rationalize that it's a game of numbers." Even when business rebounds, "Keep your image alive by being part of an organization or sending out a mailing every few months."

For steady growth, a core group of good clients are your best bet, since happy customers are your best publicity. "Most business comes from three to five good accounts. They should be called on regularly, and any referrals you can get from them is much better than a cold call," added Howard. To scout out potential clients, you'll need to make yourself visible. Networking groups, art/design shows, openings, and clubs are prime targets. If you're a natural at the microphone, you may try public speaking at industry-related committees or organizations.

Try to sell yourself without a portfolio. Call people up on the phone. Don't just e-mail them or mail them a letter. It's too easily dismissed or deleted by busy professionals. Instead, call and say that you'd like to introduce yourself. Get potential clients into a conversation and talk about what they need and want and how you can help them. Use the opportunity of personal contact not just to connect but to research the firm you're interested in.

If you resort to using marketing materials to solicit new business, you should include at least ten of your best work samples, a resume, business cards, a brochure, and a friendly letter that highlights your abilities and how they relate to a particular client's needs. Be sure to follow up your package with a call or a note. If you have an online presence, "Keep it professional, simple, and easy to navigate. Include your bio and work samples. Don't force potential customers to watch long intros, and don't expect everyone to have the latest software versions. Use it to generate interest rather than to tell your whole story. The Web site is your way of getting that client contact and a face-to-face meeting so you can introduce yourself," Howard advised. Time management is critical to succeeding at freelancing. Sometimes a few hours can make the difference between turning a profit on a job or going broke. Freelancers must be organized, disciplined self-starters who can multitask, or not much will get done. If you don't already have a handle on managing your own time, then freelancing is probably not for you. You need a more structured work environment.

The best resource for freelancers is people who have been freelancing successfully for some time. Take them out for coffee and pick their brains about how they do it. Don't ask them to get you work or pass along work that they don't have time to do. Just ask them what they would recommend in handling the areas where you need help.

After your first year freelancing, a great deal of your work should be coming from referrals. "There is nothing more valuable than a good referral for new business. References are good to have but should seldom be used, and don't bother with testimonials as they don't convince anybody of anything. Save them for funeral and wedding speeches," Howard added.

Top Twenty Sites for Locating Freelance Work

1. *www.dice.com*—Dice is a fully stocked job-search engine for high-tech professionals. Must use "freelance" as a keyword in your search. Headhunters allowed.

2. *www.workexchange.com*—Claims to be "the largest networked marketplace for project work on the Internet." Registration required. Works like an auction—job goes to the person with the best bid. Headhunters allowed.

3. *www.hireweb.com*—Registration required. No headhunters allowed. Offers internships, too.

4. *www.careerpark.com*—Covers a spectrum of industries. Search under the Part-time/Freelance category.

5. *www.guru.com*—Boasts over 18,000 hiring companies. No headhunters allowed. Mostly new media jobs.

6. *www.freeagent.com*—Covers a spectrum of industries. Registration required.

7. *www.exp.com*—Advertises itself as a service that connects individuals to experts in any of nearly 100 categories. Freelancers looking for new gigs should click on Give Advice. Registration required.

8. *www.hotjobs.com*—Perhaps the largest and most established career embankment on the Web. Covers a spectrum of industries. Must use "freelance" as a keyword in your search.

9. *www.monster.com*—Another mammoth career site. Covers a spectrum of industries. Must use "freelance" as a keyword in your search.

10. *www.freelancewriting.com*—As its name indicates, a site for working writers across various industries. Go to Freelance Job Bank & Creative Outsourcing.

11. *www.elance.com*—Covers a spectrum of industries. Registration required. Works like an auction—job goes to the person with the best bid.

12. *www.ants.com*—Covers a spectrum of industries. Registration required. Works like an auction—job goes to the person with the best bid.

13. *www.flexmind.com*—Prefers candidates who have graduated

Ivy League or the equivalent. Registration required. Works like an auction—job goes to the person with the best bid.

14. *www.freetimejobs.com*—Covers a spectrum of industries. Registration required.

15. *www.e-work.com*—Registration required. Headhunters allowed.

16. *www.tjobs.com*—Stands for telecommuting jobs. Mostly new media jobs.

17. *www.careerpath.com*—Covers a spectrum of industries. Must use "freelance" as a keyword in your search.

18. *www.netread.com*—Specifically for professionals in the publishing industry. Search under Freelance/Contract Part-Time, Freelance/Contract Full-Time, or Telecommute.

19. *www.freelancers.com*—Especially for creative freelancers or those involved in design, illustration, writing, editing, and photography.

20. *www.vault.com*—Covers a spectrum of industries. Must use freelance as a keyword in your search. Includes optional feature for excluding headhunters.

Myths and Legends

At one time or another, we've all tripped over our own two feet. Sometimes, we just don't realize when we're standing in our own way. Rich Ramsey, managing director of the New York office of career services provider Lee Hecht Harrison, is surprised at how many job seekers rule themselves out as candidates for employment prospects based on misconceptions they have about the job market.

Of the most common myths that discourage the unemployed, the most common is that there's no use applying to a company that's announced a hiring freeze. "While about half of all employers say they have a job freeze, they still do selective hiring since there are always key positions that need to be filled," said Ramsey. To find these hidden opportunities, try to connect with someone who works in a similar function. Those folks are the best information sources," he added.

Professional and industry trade groups are also hot spots for meeting company insiders. When you hear about an opening, direct your cover letter to the department or unit manager and be clear and concise about what you are able to bring to the table.

It's also wrong to think that companies that have laid off thousands of employees won't be hiring new ones. "It's standard procedure for companies to downsize their staffs in some areas, while at the same time continuing to hire in others. If you're very savvy about a particular organization's mission and their growth strategy, contact them. They will be on the lookout for those who can help them keep their costs down," Ramsey said.

Another myth that job seekers fall prey to is that big companies do more hiring than small ones. Actually, in the wake of a downturn, most new jobs in metro areas will come from medium- to small-size employers. "Also, just because you make a move to a smaller company, you don't have to lower your salary expectations. Just be willing to have more of your compensation based on your own individual production," added Ramsey.

It used to be that job seekers didn't let on when they were unemployed. This isn't so today. "Employers are sophisticated and know what's going on in the job market. It's better to be forthright and nondefensive in an interview rather than waste time trying to keep up a front," advised Ramsey. Stay positive during such meetings. "When two candidates for a job are virtually equal, hiring managers will always hire the more optimistic person," he added.

Another myth: People that don't have relationships with business leaders can't benefit from networking. "Everyone can and should network," asserts Mr. Ramsey. "Talk with as many people as possible for advice, information, and job leads. Notwithstanding the Internet job sites, most people find new employment through other people. There's no telling where that new job will come from.

The Hardest Job You'll Ever Have May Be Finding One

Those in the professional employment field say that the job hunter needs an average of 700 fresh contacts to get a job. Pretend you're heading the corporate headquarters of My Job-Hunt, Inc., and search for work as if that's your full-time job. Work at least thirty to forty hours per week on getting a new job. Divide your time between contacting potential employers and generating new leads. Don't quit until you have a written job offer in hand.

You can research potential employers using mailing lists, the Internet, and your local business yellow pages. Contact and recontact your job leads. Follow up on the resumes you send out. Change the format of your resume (functional or chronological) and resubmit it again. Resubmit resumes about every six weeks. Positions open all the time, and though companies promise to keep your resume on file, many are too awash in paper to really sort through them when they need to fill a position in a hurry.

Be a contender. On interviews, review the job's requirements with the interviewer and find out whether this is the only interview. If you're truly interested in the company or position, ask for the next interview! In today's job market, most employers will not reveal their interest unless you express yours. Exit the interview in a polite and assured manner, don't press for an early decision, and don't discuss salary, vacation, or benefits. Allow your interviewer to bring this up first.

Looking for a job is hard work, so cut yourself some slack. Don't feel guilty about taking time off from your job hunt. Just do it mindfully. If you spent Saturday at the copy shop and post office, take Tuesday off. Remember, it's all up to you. There are many excuses not to make calls or send resumes. There are no real reasons and no jobs out there for those who won't look. There are countless opportunities for those who wholeheartedly turn over the stones.

Summary

Finding work doesn't have to be the hardest job you'll ever have, if you know how to go about it. Getting a foot in the door may require persistence and a few fancy moves, but if you put in the hours of looking, it will pay dividends.

Tips to remember:

- If you are a freelancer or doing contract work and are currently successful, don't rest on your laurels. Seeking out new contacts and projects keeps your skill set fresh, your work flow steadier, and your income healthier. Regular gigs are great, but don't rely on them.
- There's an art to resume writing, and it's well worth learning. Your greatness won't be seen unless you have a solid resume to send to potential employers or clients.
- Find a mentor—someone you trust and admire to help you on your way.
- Be prepared to work hard. It will pay off.

Chapter 10

Discovering Your True Calling:
Career Ideas for Artistic Types

Finding your occupational calling can be an angst-filled process. At the very least, it involves a great deal of soul searching. After all, we invest so much of our identity in what we do professionally. Moreover, our choice of vocation directly affects our income potential, lifestyle, and even where we live. The good news is that if you already know what you like, what you're good at, and what you want to do, then you're already halfway to achieving it. But what if you only have a nagging sense of unfulfillment? Maybe your present occupation isn't awful, but it doesn't challenge you or make your heart sing. How can you determine what is missing from your life?

The Six Job Personality Types

For the past thirty years, the work of noted career theorist John Holland, Ph.D., has been used by career advisors and educators looking to match people with their ideal job path. His tried-and-true theory is pretty basic: that people are attracted to the work environments that match their personalities and backgrounds. Basically, we choose jobs that match our preconception of that occupation and that will surround us with like-minded people.

There are six kinds of work personalities: realistic, investigative, artistic, social, enterprising, and conventional. Although you may have one dominant trait, there are subtraits that affect you too. Discovering where you fit can help you see what is missing in your creative or professional life. The list below is arranged in a hexagon. You are likely to have traits in the two sections on either side of your main personality trait. You are unlikely to be strong in the trait listed directly opposite yours.

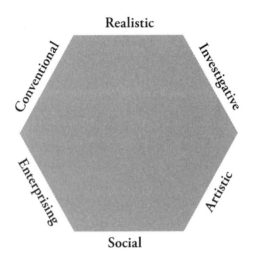

Realistic

Realistic people are good at fixing things. As well as being athletic, they may like to work with animals or in an agricultural capacity. They need to see something tangible as a result of their efforts and would rather do something than sit around talking about it. Their occupations usually require good coordination and motor skills and may have an element of competitiveness. Jobs they are drawn to include car mechanic, air traffic controller, carpenter, electrician, construction worker, farmer, firefighter, police officer, or locksmith.

Investigative

Investigative people are the brainy types who figure out how to run DOS and who understand the Pythagorean theorem. They value science and have a methodical, thorough, reasoned approach to everything they do. They are precise and detail oriented. They shy away from leadership roles and hate to participate in anything involving persuasion or sales. Investigative people may not have particularly good people skills. They prefer to think rather than to act. Jobs for these people include biologist, mathematician, architect, chemist, physicist, anthropologist, geologist, pharmacist, veterinarian, doctor (if they cross over into a people skilled group), and medical technologist.

Artistic

Artistic people include all the creative types—artists, actors, sculptors, authors, and musicians. They are talented and expressive and have original and independent thought processes. They value self-expression and are likely to be emotional. They are not too dissimilar from investigative types; however, artistic types are unlikely to flourish in environments requiring strict attention to detail or within a confined work code. Their job paths tend to be challenging—acting, drama, writing, and designing—though there are many variations of these creative roles.

Social

Social people like to help, and they are hands-on in their practicality. They are the teachers, counselors, nurses, and social workers of our society, as well as our religious and spiritual leaders. They are unlikely to enjoy working with machines and much prefer to be around people. They are helpful, friendly, and trustworthy in personality. Other jobs that would interest them are physical therapist, athletic trainer, dental hygienist, or parole officer.

Enterprising

Enterprising people are leaders, politicians, and entrepreneurs. They like to express their opinions and are energetic and ambitious.

They don't enjoy overanalyzing situations, preferring to be swept up by enthusiasm and drive. They enjoy people and tend to be sociable. Jobs for these types include anything in sales and management, travel agent, lawyer, realtor, television or film producer, sports promoter, and banking.

Conventional

Conventional people like to crunch numbers. They value success in business and are unlikely to take monetary risks. They are systematic in their approach to work and can follow a plan of action to the letter. They dislike unstructured activities. Jobs for them include accountant, secretary, bookkeeper, court clerk, mail carrier, tax expert, or financial analyst.

By finding out your traits, you can see whether you are in the right job, whether you should consider a career move, or narrow down areas that are not being fulfilled in your life for either a second or parallel career.

To find out your traits, complete the survey below, being as honest as you can with your answers. Ask people close to you about their opinions, too, as their ideas about your personality may differ (perhaps you are less sociable or more mechanically minded than you think!).

When you have completed the survey, add up your scores. Take the initial from the group with the most checked answers (for example: R for Realistic), then take the initial from the next group where you checked the most answers. This will give you the two initials that will identify your career major and minor.

Check the statements that best describe you.

REALISTIC

❏ I'm very practical
❏ I'm good at building and fixing things

❒ I like to tinker with mechanical things
❒ I like to play sports
❒ I'm good at solving problems
❒ I prefer to work outdoors
❒ I'm very straightforward
❒ I can pitch a tent
❒ I'm competitive
❒ I can read a blueprint
❒ I can operate tools and machinery
❒ I enjoy gardening

INVESTIGATIVE

❒ I'm inquisitive
❒ I like to explore different ideas
❒ I'm good at math
❒ I am able to analyze data
❒ I think abstractly
❒ I'm very computer savvy
❒ I understand physical theories
❒ I prefer to work independently
❒ I'm observant
❒ I'm very precise and detail oriented
❒ I can operate tools and machinery
❒ I like to work on mechanical things

ARTISTIC

❒ I like to sketch, draw, paint, sculpt, or write
❒ I like to go to concerts, theaters, or art exhibits
❒ I'm very intuitive
❒ I can play a musical instrument
❒ I read a lot of fiction, plays, or poetry
❒ I have a lot of imagination
❒ I like to sing, act, or dance

- ❐ I like doing craft projects
- ❐ I like redesigning my home's interior
- ❐ I like taking photographs
- ❐ I'm an individualist
- ❐ I tend to be emotional

SOCIAL

- ❐ I'm good at teaching or training others
- ❐ I prefer to work around other people
- ❐ I can express myself well
- ❐ I like helping people with their problems
- ❐ I'm very outgoing
- ❐ I can lead a group discussion
- ❐ I can mediate disputes
- ❐ I cooperate well with others
- ❐ I'm good at planning and supervising
- ❐ I'm very understanding
- ❐ I enjoy team sports
- ❐ I do volunteer work

ENTERPRISING

- ❐ I'm very assertive
- ❐ I like to take control and do things my way
- ❐ I'm very self-confident
- ❐ I'm comfortable making decisions that affect others
- ❐ I can convince people to my way of thinking
- ❐ I can sell things or promote ideas
- ❐ I'm comfortable giving talks or speeches
- ❐ I have lots of energy
- ❐ I'm good at organizing activities and events
- ❐ I tend to be the group leader
- ❐ I'm very enthusiastic
- ❐ I enjoy meeting important people

CONVENTIONAL
- ❒ I prefer to follow clearly defined procedures
- ❒ I'm always well groomed
- ❒ I'm very detail oriented
- ❒ I can do a lot of paper work in a short time
- ❒ I like to work with numbers
- ❒ I'm computer savvy
- ❒ I can use data processing programs
- ❒ I write effective business letters
- ❒ I'm very conscientious and have a great work ethic
- ❒ I'm very efficient
- ❒ My work is always very accurate
- ❒ I work in a methodical way

Combining Your Talents

The range of creative jobs is vast, with different skill sets needed for each one. Once you've determined your areas, you need to find a path that you will be happy to travel. Here are fifty of the top jobs that can help put you on the road to creative fulfillment.

Advertising art director

The coveted role of the ad art director is challenging and important. As the person responsible for the look of a print ad, you must be extremely creative and able to work under pressure. The ability to maintain a steady, creative working relationship with a copywriter is tantamount, since the two of you in tandem are creating the identity of the product or company. As a team, art directors and copywriters develop and design advertising campaigns based on demographic market research. This information helps them decide at which kind of audience they should aim their campaign. They then apply their creative intuition and imagination to finding original ways to execute their advertising. Once developed, the campaign is typically approved by the account executive and creative director before being presented to the client for final approval. The art director executes the final ad by selecting the type and illustration. A successful team can be responsible for creating pop culture itself—after all, how many slogans and instantly recognizable ad icons do you know?

Album cover designer

Although the advent of CDs has taken away some of the thrilling aspects that used to come with the territory of record album design, this is still a highly creative area. The designer needs to be a good graphic designer, but must also give a visual equivalent of the mood of the music. A design decision is arrived at with the input of the record company sales department, usually respecting the ideas and wishes of the featured recording artist. This person must be aware of the current musical trends in all musical genres as well as youth and pop culture.

Architectural photographer

An architectural photographer is specifically skilled at photographing buildings and interiors. Aside from often being works of art in themselves, the photographs are used for annual reports and trade magazines. Architects often need photographs of work in progress, taken from all angles. Home magazines like *House and Garden* or *Living* often publish photographs by architectural photographers, as do art and architectural publications.

Art/music therapist

Not all talented art and music students want to isolate themselves in a studio, so if you're an artist who loves to be sociable and help people, this is the job for you. To take this on, though, you will need to have a lot of patience. The therapy can be used for people who want to explore their psyche, or it can be as part of a broader treatment, headed by a psychiatrist, for those who have experienced trauma or are emotionally disturbed. Such professionals work with people of all ages who have varying degrees of functional or physical impairment. They may work with individuals or groups and even within families. Work usually takes place in private psychiatric hospitals and clinics, mental health centers, geriatric centers, and prisons. Other work is in private or public schools and institutions for the emotionally disturbed or with deaf, blind, or otherwise physically challenged people. A few therapists work with the physically ill and even with terminal patients. It can be challenging but extremely gratifying work.

Both music and art can be extraordinarily therapeutic, helping people to uncover and release ideas and feeling they are otherwise unable to express, as well as with the restoration, maintenance, and improvement of mental and physical health.

Animator

The movie business is booming, and with the success of companies like Pixar, as well as the advent of Japanese anime, there's a need for highly creative and technologically savvy folks. And not just in the movies. Animators are also being employed by the gaming software industry, as well as businesses that want to use simulations for presentations, to speed up business functions, and enhance their bottom lines. For example, architectural firms, such as those who presented redesign ideas for the World Trade Center, used three-dimensional computer modeling to simulate internal and external environments of building developments. Instead of manually preparing drawings, landscapers and interior decorators are hiring freelance animators to design virtual sketches for their clients, giving them a realistic look and feel for their design plans. Insurance firms work with animators to produce reenactments of collisions and accidents. Automotive firms simulate concept cars, and telecommunication companies design cell phones. And companies large and small are enhancing their Web presence and identity using animation for logo design.

Most animators go from project to project, working at postproduction houses or for in-house graphics departments of cable networks. There's abundant work for postproduction houses and in-house graphics departments for cable networks such as HBO or CNN.

Living the Dream

Yvette Vega, film director/yoga instructor

Yvette Vega has used her gift for documentary filmmaking to turn her own personal tragedy into one of evolution and professional growth. At just twelve years old, without warning, she lost her older sister to a brain aneurism. Throughout her twenties, Yvette gained strength from working in the fitness industry. She traveled all over Latin America as a certification specialist and was discovered for her first television role on the Family Channel's Cable Health Club, an internationally syndicated program. She loved the filmmaking process so much that she raised $20,000 in sponsorships and negotiated a distribution contract for a series of Latin-dance, aerobics videos, which she produced, starred in, and turned a profit from. Her exposure to different healing practices, including an Oriental/Egyptian style dance called Beledi, helped to ease the pain of her sister's untimely death by helping the body open energy centers and purge painful emotions. Yvette's personal catharsis is actually paving the way for new career milestones. She recently made her directorial debut with "Healing Death." The documentary work weaves story telling with artists, poets, and singers who bravely share and perform the art that helped them to heal after the loss of a loved one. "I want to develop my craft and be an agent of change. It's about creating your own possibilities," she said.

While starting salaries in New York and Los Angeles range between $30K and $50K, if you go "Hollywood," animation directors at movie studios rake in anywhere from $75K to $200K depending on geographical location.

Antique furniture restorers and finishers

The work consists of repairing antique furniture by replacing missing or broken parts and finishing or refinishing furniture. You need to be highly detail oriented, have a steady hand, and be able to confidently work on sometimes very valuable pieces. Antique furniture restorers and finishers may work for museums, or they can start their own small business or contract out to antique dealers or insurance companies should a client's antiques by damaged by fire or flood. They usually have artistic and technical skills, as well as business skills in money management and communication.

Book jacket designer

When browsing for a book, there are three things that are available to the merchandiser to get the attention of a shopper—a famous author, a snappy title, or a great-looking book cover. A good book jacket design may use type alone or work in conjunction with photography or illustration. The book jacket designer needs a strong sense of design and knowledge of the latest developments in typography and lettering. The artist may be employed by a publisher or a studio specializing in book jacket design or may work on a freelance basis.

Cartoonist

Cartoons range in scope from one-frame funnies in the newspaper to incredibly crafted full-color art books. Cartoons can be art, social commentary, an illustrated novel, or simply entertainment.

For comics such as Superman or Batman, the comic creation is multifaceted. It consists primarily of a penciler and an inker, although a letterer and a colorist may also contribute. By far, the penciler is considered to have the greatest creative input—he's the one that must come up with the inspiration for the drawing and initiate the creative process. The inker then adds the depth and finesse to the drawing.

Mostly, comic strips are owned by a syndicate (a publisher of features that makes a number of titles available to newspapers worldwide). The artist who draws, writes, or creates a title is basically a contract employee. There are freelance positions, too, and of course those who have creations that go on to fortune and fame (like *The Simpsons*) are afforded a very nice lifestyle.

Comic art is also used in Web site applications and magazine and book design, and with the popularity of cartoons, not only in and of themselves, but as the basis for movies and TV shows (see Animators), cartooning is a growing field. Aspiring cartoonists need superb drawing skills, coupled with the ability to tell a story through art. Motivation is important, since it can be a solitary occupation at times, and there can be setbacks, such as being commissioned to do a sketch or a more detailed drawing that is never published.

Copywriter

Copywriters are the wordsmiths behind ads—the people who come up with the snappy titles and then grab the consumer with their rhetoric. They need to be able to come up with imaginative ideas and work well with a design team. The copywriter creates the words that accompany the pictures in print advertisements as well as the voiceover words for television visuals. The copywriter is expected to come up with concepts that include both copy and visuals either alone or in tandem with an art director. As such, it helps if a copywriter has a great design sense—in fact, copywriters are not necessarily writers. Often some of the best copywriters have backgrounds in commercial art. It is useful for a copywriter to know the ins and outs of print production (newspapers, magazines, and annual reports) as well as the production aspects of film, radio, and video tape.

Costume designer

Using fashion-design skills, costume designers create apparel for actors and actresses in TV, movies, and the theater. With keen knowledge of fashion history, from ancient times to recent fashion, they are able to create authentic and realistic costumes. Whatever the media, the costume designer must know all that a fashion designer must know and then some. Vast historical knowledge is needed, as well the necessary skills to research when needed, in order to accurately reconstruct costumes of various historical periods. Sometimes the costume designer is called upon to create highly imaginative, innovative costuming, in science fiction or fantasy pieces, for example, and in this respect they must be able to invent new ways of structuring costumes. Ideas must be sketched first so that they may be understood by pattern makers and machinists.

Critic

Feel like everyone's a critic? If you have excellent knowledge of a subject and can write with authority, you could be the one giving the thumbs up or down. Subjects such as music (from pop to opera or jazz), stage and movie productions, and painting, sculpture, and other arts require specialist journalists to cover them for the press. Aside from reviewing, critics also interview well-known personalities within the genre. A bachelor's degree in the social sciences along with at least one language and a background in subjects such as art history, communication studies, journalism, and drama is desirable. This career can be very stressful since you often have to work with tight deadlines, and you should be able to handle pressure. You should also be able to take criticism yourself, since your thoughts and reviews won't always be popular with others.

Cultural events planner

Ever wonder who puts on your local Puerto Rican parade or Caribbean arts festival? If you appreciate the role of the arts in a community, have excellent communication skills, and can relate to diverse groups of people, this could be the job for you. As an administrator, you'll manage artistic and cultural venues such as theaters and art galleries. You may be required to get sponsorship and funding through state, local, and political bodies and industry organizations, prepare and submit funding requests, and negotiate with artists and performers. You will be in charge of the events' sound and lighting, stage management and security, box office sales, distribution and sales of publications, public relations, and catering. In larger organizations, you may specialize in one particular area, such as marketing, education, or fundraising.

Dance instructor

Dance instructors are often former performers and in certain areas, like ballet, have completed significant training. Young students will look to their teachers to possibly coach them into a professional career, whether in dancing or acting, so a high degree of proficiency and know-how is essential. Other students will be there for fitness or recreation, so there should also be a fun element. Teachers must excel at dancing, be exceptionally good with people (especially children), and be able to choreograph. They need patience and good communication skills. Teachers will often explain the history and origins of the dance technique as well as introduce music concepts and be knowledgeable about physical education. Work may be found at local dance studios, schools, or therapeutic settings within hospitals.

Ecotourism/luxury travel agent

With leisure time at a premium, travelers are now much more savvy and demanding in their choices of destinations and vacation plans. They are willing to look and pay for help in finding the right fit for their lifestyle. For these clients, travel tends to be culturally focused. For ecotourists, it may be a question of seeking out places off the beaten track, where visitors may encounter wildlife or natural phenomena. For the luxury traveler, only the finest accommodations suffice, and travelers usually fly first or business class. They seek expert guides and high-quality vehicle transportation. Maybe they are interested in taking a cooking class given by a gourmet chef from a particularly culinary-rich country, or perhaps they are interested in exploring an area known for art and artifacts. Salary varies but can include great perks, including free travel.

Living the Dream

Ken Fish, owner, AbsoluteAsia.com

While working for an Australian-based travel firm in the 1980s, Ken Fish had the opportunity to travel extensively on that side of the equator, including to parts of Southeast Asia. When he returned to the United States, impassioned by his experiences, Fish conceptualized his vision of a company that would offer quality, privately guided tour services to the Asia-Pacific region.

Fish officially realized his business idea and founded his luxury tour operator company in 1989. Today, the company boasts an array of tour offerings to places such as Thailand, Malaysia, and New Zealand. The process of custom tailoring every trip is highly personalized. "It may take two or three revisions of an itinerary before it's finalized," he said. While deluxe travel doesn't come cheap, the extra dollars go a long way when it comes to the X-factors that can often make or break a trip. "We're always monitoring the political and social conditions throughout Asia. Unless there's a particular crisis and safety is an issue, it is very rare that we will interrupt service to a destination. The rewards of his career are fairly simple to pinpoint. "When someone comes back and tells you about the once-in-a-lifetime experience you planned for them, it's extremely fulfilling."

Living the Dream

Barbara Franco, publisher, SeasonedCitizen.com

After coming home from her full-time job, New York-based resident Barbara Franco began publishing a local, monthly print newspaper called "The Seasoned Citizen." It targeted the fifty-five plus, savvy senior population and was supported by neighborhood advertisers. "The circular quickly caught on, and, after an eight-year run, we had hit a monthly circulation of 20,000." With this impressive level of success, Ms. Franco expanded her horizons, and in October 1998 she brought her newspaper online. Visitors to her Web site (which is no longer active) could access feature articles from any of the publication's prime "content channels," which included health, travel and leisure, money matters, and legal advice. According to Ms. Franco, "The feedback was overwhelmingly encouraging."

The Web site has been listed as a top site for seniors on the Internet's most popular search engines, including Yahoo, Excite, and Lycos. Aside from banner advertisers, Ms. Franco incorporated other revenue streams, marketing partnerships, and alliances with companies that sell products and services to this explosive market.

E-magazine editor/reporter

Despite the bust of the dot-coms, online publishing is still a hot industry, since people are increasingly turning to the Web for information and news. To break into the field, you must understand "Web time." As an online reporter or editor, you may need to update your magazine's site as often as ten or more times daily. You need to be able to write and present your work concisely, as greater volumes of information must be condensed into a much smaller space. The number of jobs available in this field is increasing because many smaller ventures and not just mainstream brand magazines are making a presence for themselves on the Web. With this low-cost opportunity to reach an international audience, even smaller publishers and entrepreneurs are now able to get into the act.

Event planner

Making sure an event goes seamlessly requires both skill and hard work. Planners have to meet with trade and professional associations to promote and discuss their event or conference needs. This involves budgeting, meeting with organizing committees, and coordinating services such as transport, conference facilities, catering, accommodation, signs, displays, translation, audio-visual equipment, security, and special needs requirements. On top of that, the planner must organize the guest list and/or registration of participants, prepare programs, and occasionally also publicize the event. Most planners begin by working with a large company, but if you start up on your own, you will also need to be able to hire, train, and supervise support staff (bar staff, doormen, security), ensure compliance with relevant by-laws, negotiate contracts, maintain financial records, and review the final billing.

Exhibit and museum display designer

Depending on the type of display, the designer may well need specific knowledge of the subjects involved. For instance, with educational displays (archeology, paleontology, Egyptology, and the like), the layout and order of the material is essential to understanding the piece. Art museums also have their own skill and knowledge requirements. For other types of display, such as those for conventions, exhibits, and department stores, both inside and outdoors, basic knowledge of graphic design, type, lettering, and color is needed as well. Drafting, model building, and carpentry skills are useful. In all cases, an understanding of architectural design is helpful, particularly in determining how best to move people through the display.

Living the Dream

Regina McMenamin, president, Regina Ink Ltd.

For this one-woman event planner, every day is just another celebration. "I love wine, food, and the type of people who go to restaurants," she said. While working for a major New York ad firm, she landed a career-changing client, The Four Seasons Restaurant of Manhattan. As her employer's prime liaison to the legendary eatery, Regina designed invites, produced wine dinners, and composed witty ads on the spot. She also wrote clever, amusing thank-you memos and congratulatory notes to patrons such as Henry Kissinger, Heidi Klum, and Ralph Lauren. Her flair for catering to the rich and famous paid off. She struck out on her own. Today, her billings exceed $20,000 a month. Clients include The World Bar, St. Francis Wines, and The National Parks of New York Harbor. Her typical workday may entail coordinating a $500-a-plate wine dinner, a fashion show, a film screening, or a cocktail party, or even ghostwriting a book. She boasts a who's who database of 7,000 people, organized by food and wine preferences and dating likes and dislikes. "I want people to have a good time whether they're a regular twenty-two-year-old or sixty-five-year-old billionaire," she said. Looking ahead, Regina would like to pen her own novel about the inside drama of restaurants.

Facility education coordinator

An education coordinator designs educational programs for museums, zoos, galleries, and other educational facilities. They prepare lectures for visiting groups, assist staff in giving guided tours, and participate in book tours, lectures, and related activities. Interested applicants need a BA in education or a related field, and some museum or library experience may be required. Graduate work in library sciences, museum studies, new media technologies, art history, or education is highly desirable.

Fashion accessories designer

If you are adept at identifying fashion trends, particularly in hard goods and accessories such as wallets, handbags, shoes, belts, and travel gear, consider this career avenue. You should be able to design product ideas based off of sketches. You'll also need to be comfortable designing for a variety of fabrics, from leather to metal. You'll be expected to work with management, vendors, merchandisers, and sales force on product design, development, and presentation.

Fashion designer

Are you the next Armani or Dior? The road to fashion greatness is a tough one, and you have to pay your dues to get ahead in this cutthroat business. Fashion designers are the artists of the apparel industry. They create clothing design ideas for a range of products, including coats, dresses, hats, handbags, swimwear, lingerie, shoes, and underwear. Yet they also have to be able to understand technical details, such as fabric qualities, from durability to feel and use. They study the construction of garments from start to finish and are experienced with fabric printing and print design, sketching for the designer and illustrator, industry-standard pattern drafting, showroom and retail sales, fashion history, textiles, computerized design, and merchandising and marketing. Aside from careers with the top names in the industry, there are many fashion designers working in-house for department-store lines, for textile, apparel, or pattern manufacturers, or for wholesale distributors or retailers. Some designers are self-employed and work with individual clients.

Living the Dream

Keiko, designer, Keiko Swimwear

For years, Keiko's suits have adorned models on the covers of *Sports Illustrated*, *Self*, *Maxim*, *Shape*, and *Muscle & Fitness*. Born and raised in Tokyo, Japan, as a girl Keiko learned much about the fashion design craft from her mother, a dressmaker. At age nineteen, Keiko trekked to the United States and, supporting herself as a waitress, studied at the School of Visual Arts in New York and later in Paris. By 1972, she had designed her own contemporary sportswear collection, which was carried by Gimbel's Department Store, a huge deal for an up-and-coming designer. Throughout the 1980s, with more help from investors, Keiko's designer swimwear lined the racks of Macy's and Saks Fifth Avenue. "My backer went out of business and suddenly we didn't have a showroom." Fed up with having to seek out another partner, she went solo. Today, Keiko wears both the designer's and the manufacturer's hats. Aside from her Manhattan store, she picks and chooses the boutiques she sells to, which include the swim shops of luxury hotels and resorts. She credits her patience and listening skills for much of her success, adding that feedback has helped her adapt her product line. "I listen to what customers want, what their problems are, and I solve them," she said.

Feng shui adviser

This ancient Chinese system teaches how to create harmony between nature and manmade structures, and offices and employers are increasingly adopting its teachings as they look toward creating greater harmony in the workplace. In the home, people are also using the basics of feng shui to create a better living space and more visually appealing rooms. Today's experts are hired to do consultations for both residential and commercial spaces—from home offices to large retail establishments. Income potential is huge, but it does require that you know your stuff and get good guidance and training from a feng shui expert.

Living the Dream

Ileen Nelson, feng shui practitioner

Ileen Nelson discovered her calling as a feng shui practitioner eight years ago. After reading a few intriguing books on the subject, she employed some of the principles to her own home. "My husband had grown dissatisfied at work, complaining that he wasn't earning enough," she recalled. Nelson noticed that her children's swing set was situated in the "wealth section" of her property. To better maximize her family's luck and fortune, Nelson moved the swing set and added more lighting, a coin collection, and red-colored objects (which stimulate *chi*, or life force). Her healing home improvements paid off. "Within a month, my husband was promoted to national sales manager for his company," said Nelson. Fascinated with the results, Nelson took a continuing education course in feng shui and went on to get certified in the subject. She later opened up the Long Island Feng Shui Institute to offer a range of educational and professional certificate programs for those interested in this field. Students can even become more specialized and earn certificates on particular feng shui subjects such as Space Clearing, Selling Your House, and Marketing Yourself.

Film location scout

When a movie or TV production company requires a certain type of location—a Midwest suburban street scene, say, or a deserted beach—the scout is responsible for coming up with a list of possibilities. Film location scouts visit the area, contact location owners, prepare locations, assist in negotiating deals, communicate with neighborhoods, prepare location documents, and arrange for location equipment. You will also need to know how to work within the confines and restrictions of the film company and the budget. As with any career in the motion picture industry, you'll often work irregular hours to meet tight schedules. The ability to work well in a team environment and handle stress well are essential skills.

Floral designer

Being in charge of the flowers for people's life-changing events is a big responsibility, and it takes creativity and flair. While some floral designers work for an established flower shop, many others end up running their own businesses. They design and deliver bouquets, corsages, swags, garlands, arrangements, and wreaths for occasions such as birthdays, anniversaries, funerals, parties, and banquets.

If you want to own your own shop, you also need skills in window dressing and in-store displays. If you have a knack for line, form, space, and depth in floral design and a talent for grouping shapes, proportions, and colors together, you could be cut out for this challenging job. Knowledge of texture and fragrance is important in this line of work as well. Or you may choose to specialize in artificial flowers, Oriental arrangements, or flowers to wear as wristlets, barrettes, corsages, and boutonnieres.

Greeting card creator

Every year, to express our softer emotional sides, Americans send roughly 2.1 billion cards—and that's just during the Christmas holiday season. Hallmark and American Greetings dominate the market, and while employment at these two companies is very competitive, roughly 2,000 other smaller publishers provide opportunities. In addition, the rising popularity of electronic greeting cards has opened up new prospects for artists and writers.

Hairstylist

Hairstylists have to be continually creative—they need to be able to serve clients all day long and still turn out excellent work, down to the last customer. They need to have excellent people and communication skills, as well as be a good listener and impromptu therapist! The profession can be physically tiring after standing up for long hours, but the work can be fun, and for those at the top of their game, lucrative. To become a hairstylist, you first need to become a licensed cosmetologist, which means completing roughly 1,000 hours of beauty school study, at the end of which you must pass a written and practical state-licensing exam. Depending on where you practice your trade, you may need to perform hair cutting, coloring, and styling, along with manicuring, aesthetics (facials, etc.), waxing, and other beauty services. New hairstylists often start with menial tasks while learning on the job from the experienced stylists, sometimes also attending salon schools such as those run by Vidal Sassoon. The best hairstylists stay abreast of current trends and developments in cutting and styling techniques and products. While base salaries are often low, especially to start, tips can be substantial, and the really top stylists can write their own ticket, especially if they go on to open their own successful salon.

Imagineer

The expansion of theme parks and the thirst for high-quality entertainment facilities means there is a need for people who can dream up roller coasters, rides, and attractions and make them work. It's a tough field requiring a lot of creativity, technical know-how, and immense attention to detail. The Walt Disney Company came up with the name Imagineer to describe their 2,000-strong crack team of employees, representing over 140 disciplines, who are responsible for all phases of their theme-park project development. Imagineering is the master planning, creative development, design, engineering, production, project management, and research and development arm of company. The talented corps of Imagineers are responsible for the creation—from concept initiation through installation—of all Disney resorts, theme parks, and attractions, real-estate developments, regional entertainment venues, and new media projects. It's a hard job to get into, and there is no set career path, but for those that fit the bill, it's a highly rewarding and motivating job. Doug Wolf, project manager of Walt Disney Imagineering in Florida, gives this advice: "Dream and pursue your imagination and goals. Do anything that stirs your creativity—read, write, draw, observe, and travel. Learn what you enjoy and excel at, whether it be model building, drawing, writing, or construction. See if there's a fit. Most likely there is since Imagineering encompasses almost everything imaginable. But above all, enjoy what paths your life travels and learn from each experience." Imagineering is headquartered in Glendale, California (see Resources for details).

Interactive advertising copywriter

You'll be responsible for generating breakthrough ideas and brainstorming with art directors and designers to create concepts for online ads. Aside from knowing how to create the technical imagery, writing great headlines and copy should come naturally, too. The ideas you think up should be user friendly and reflect the way everyday people transact online.

Jingle writer

You may find them irritating, but a good jingle will stick in the mind and sell a product—sometimes more than any other part of a commercial. Jingle writers are commissioned and hired to write effective jingles, not songs. Unlike songwriting, when writing a jingle, you have as little as fifteen seconds to make your point. The majority of jingles are produced by advertising agencies and specialist jingle production companies. Many use freelance writers on an individual project basis. It's a competitive field, where persistence and originality pay off. You need to prepare a demo demonstrating a range of styles to show the listener you are capable of writing and producing any type of music. But if you shine in one particular style, let it come to the fore. A good jingle writer will be frequently hired, so it's a foot-in-the-door situation.

Living the Dream

Barbara Loots, greeting card writer, Hallmark, Inc.

In her thirty-plus years with Hallmark, Barbara Loots has helped millions of Americans renew and affirm connections with people. A word stylist in the company's Writing Collaboratory, her passion for words began as a child. The daughter of a military officer, Ms. Loots was regularly uprooted to different parts of the world. "I had a need to connect with people in my past and with anyone I met. I learned to make friends quickly and cherish the moment. The urge to write letters became an overwhelming force in my life," she said. While she considers herself warmhearted, "The main thing [as a greeting card writer] is to be real. People can detect phoniness a mile a way," she said. When drafting card verses, Ms. Loots said she doesn't write for *everybody*, she writes for *somebody*. "There's a giver and a receiver. Emotions are so universal. If I can feel it, you can feel it," she said.

Landscape architect

If you have a great visual sense, as well as good knowledge of plants, and love the outdoors, this is the job for you. Landscape architects may well work on private residences, but they don't just design for people's back yards. They also use natural elements such as land, trees, and shrubs to create attractive settings for buildings, highways, and parks. They need to be creative in order to solve sometimes quite complex design problems. But they also need practical knowledge about plants, soils, climate, construction techniques, and materials. The work is quite technical, however. After consulting with the client (or corporation), the architect is responsible for the site assessment (taking note of the physical and environmental features of a location) and must have a keen understanding of how people will be using the space. It's important to be able to create highly detailed designs of the site, showing features such as trees, shrubs, gardens, lighting, walkways, patios, decks, benches, fences, retaining walls, and fountains. As well as preparing site plans, the architect must generate reports, sketches, models, photographs, maps, land use studies, and design plans. On top of that, a landscape architect must be able to estimate the cost of each project and possibly seek local permits for work that's going to be undertaken. The architect must also allow for the preservation and recreation of historical sites, as well as manage and supervise the landscape construction work.

Most landscape architects are self-employed, while the rest work in private architectural firms or businesses that provide landscaping services. A bachelor's, master's, doctorate, or professional degree is necessary, and studies are likely to include courses in ecology, landscape plants, urban design, graphic communication, planting design, and the history and theory of landscape architecture.

Magazine art designer

A magazine's design is tantamount to its success on the stands. Not only is the designer responsible for preparing the magazine for publication, but along with the editor, he or she is involved with creating a voice and identity for the publication.

For every issue of the publication, the designer must assess the material to be included and organize it visually. This includes choosing different fonts, illustrations, photographs, and special graphic elements.

In order to develop a design concept, the designer must know the way the competition looks and create enough design differences to distinguish their publication from the crowd. Sometimes, depending on the type of magazine, designers can evolve cutting-edge work that borders on true art. But at all times, designers must be aware of their audience and prepare the work in a way that will attract and speak to them. One of the most important elements of any magazine is its cover, and the designer will devote a good deal of time and energy to choosing photos, illustrations, and/or graphics that will make it eye-catching on the stands. In addition, a designer may assign the photography, design promotional items, or assist advertisers in designing their ads. To pursue this field you should have a degree in graphic design, with training in design conception and computer layout.

Makeup artist

Can you make someone look like Marilyn Monroe or Franken-stein? Can you make a bride look blushing, without giving away that she has even a trace of makeup on? Makeup artists work for model agencies and photographers, for the theater, film, print ads, or the television industry, as well as for private clients. Makeup demands are different depending on which path you take. On TV, newscasters must look professional and natural under the studio lights; outside broadcasters must look natural despite the weather or lighting; celebrity guests will want to look glamorous. In film, you could be called upon to recreate a certain look of an era or undertake special effects. Usually, makeup is taught using the traditional method of apprenticeship. Working within major cosmetics firms, such as Revlon, a good makeup artist can build up the knowledge and expertise to work within the media or as an independent consultant.

Mural designer

More businesses are decorating their lobbies with elaborate murals, often employing trompe l'oeil techniques (literally, "to fool the eye") so that blank or dark spaces can be made to look like a garden or a beach. Thanks to a huge growth in the interest in interior design, people are demanding more individualized decorating within their home. Faux effects and creative paint techniques are in vogue, and the market is booming. Interior decorators, therefore, are becoming a good source of contacts for painters. Excellent painting technique is required, with an eye for detail and a knack for color concepts. One should approach this field with an education in fine art and art history.

Music composer

Original music is needed for many medias, from commercials to plays, to TV theme tunes and movie scores. Composers generally start as musicians and go on to outsource their compositions to other artists. Composers often write works on commission or may apply for grant and competition money to pay for new works. They may also arrange, adapt, or transcribe the work of other composers. Once you are known, work is likely to be consistent and well paid, but to get to the top of the field, you must, in addition to having talent, be able to self-promote and network.

Package designer

Given a choice between two similar products, consumers will head for the one that appeals to them the most. Oftentimes that appeal comes from the packaging, including the container and the label. The ability to create new and different ways to package things is important, and the package designer must also be familiar with production and printing methods. It's also important to know which types of materials can be used with specific contents and know how to use color and type for maximum effect in attracting a consumer to a product. It may be necessary to relate the package design to the nature of the product inside. Precision drawing with tools and excellent lettering skills are required.

Photo studio manager

Studio managers must organize the scheduling and needs of the photographer and, therefore, have to be detail oriented and able to multitask. People who use the studio include magazine editors, advertising agencies, museums, and galleries. Studios are used for a wide range of assignment work, including reportage, fashion, national ad campaigns, and book projects. Duties typically include office management, invoice production and estimates, fees/sales negotiation, oversight of fine-art print production, production coordination, and management of the photo archives.

Recording studio engineer

Engineers are responsible for capturing the performances of musicians and vocalists and turning them into a high-quality audio recording. It is a highly creative, technical job, which requires great attention to detail. You need to be dedicated and have broad knowledge of various musical styles. You must have an understanding of the physics of sound, knowledge of music, good ears, patience, and technical know-how. There is a certain amount of manual work involved in the setting up of microphones, amplifiers, and gear. The engineer needs to operate all of the recording equipment and controls, including the recording console, computers, and recording software. These technical skills must be learned at a specialist school and then are usually followed by internships or an apprenticeship. Work schedules vary widely depending on the job, but long workdays, sixty to eighty hours per week, are the norm. Good engineers become well known in the industry and are much in demand, often setting up their own studios.

Satellite radio music/programming

Satellite radio is a vast network of radio stations that brings commercial-free radio channels to music lovers of every genre, as well as sports, news, and entertainment content. If you love music and have a naturally good ear, as a music programmer you decide who gets a break by being given the opportunity of radio play. As program director, you will oversee overall on-air presentation, which includes everything from music to DJs to the station's jingles. During your workday, you will be responsible for sampling new records, deciding which material fits into your station's format, and adding it to the playlist. You'll be in charge of the acquiring, cataloging, digitizing, and scheduling of music programming on assigned channels. You should be highly competitive, passionate about music, and prepared to work very hard. Other assets in this industry include business savvy and determination. You should also be able to thrive in a hectic, fast-paced, results- and delivery-oriented environment.

Screenwriter

This is just one of the jobs that many people think they can do, but very few actually can. Aside from the lure of an Oscar, having your work portrayed on screen is a thrilling concept. Writing screenplays is one of the highest paying jobs a writer can get, though like any writing, there are many who try and few who succeed. You'll need to know how to structure and create powerful plots (theme, setting, acts, scenes, etc.), characters, and most importantly, dialogue. In order to get your work read, you must also speak to agents and other writers, as well as come up with ways of promoting your work. You can submit your scripts to independent producers, but you may want to take advice from an entertainment lawyer regarding copyrights and contracts.

Set designer

A set designer is not unlike an interior designer, but must also have excellent visualization skills in order to create truly lifelike or creative, inspiring sets. They must also have technical knowledge in order to construct certain mechanical parts that enable the sets to glide on and off stage between scenes. Before creating the final stage sets, the artist must show the ideas as sketches and models. The artist must have knowledge of drawing, plan drafting, painting, model building, carpentry, and lighting. The ideas need to be expressed clearly enough for directors, costume designers, producers, lighting designers, and carpenters to understand them. The set designer must also supervise the physical construction and the painting of sets.

Living the Dream

Joe O'Donoghue, owner, Ice Fantasies

From his huge underground studio in the heart of Brooklyn, New York, Joe O'Donoghue's renowned ice-sculpting company arguably creates the coolest artwork in the neighborhood. An average ice sculpture takes three hours to "temper" and five hours of sculpting time. His creations are stored in his oversized freezer until they're shipped. Commissioned for weddings, fashion shoots, televised events, and other special occasions, Joe's frozen designs range from seahorses to rams to cartoon characters, all selling for $600 a block. Rosie O'Donnell, David Letterman, and Martha Stewart have each showcased Joe's frosty designs on their television programs. Joe even received an Emmy for the sculptures he created for the Salt Lake City Olympic games.

Sculptor

If you are truly hands on with your art, you may decide to focus on the world of sculpture. In many ways, this is one of the hardest art forms to succeed in, since the mediums for sculpting can be hard to work with, and it can sometimes involve a great deal of physical labor. Sculptors can work in clay, glass, stone, metal, sand, or wood, to name just a few mediums, and depending on the chosen form's size and substance, you can set up a studio or work out of your home. You will need to devote much of your time to self-promotion—having studio sales or calling on galleries with a portfolio of your work (remember, though, that galleries typically charge a commission of up to 50 percent). You may also apply for grants and enter competitions.

Store visual manager

Creating a great shop front and store makes the difference between getting customers to walk in off the street and having your merchandise ignored. The visual manager is responsible for creating the props and the theater in which merchandise will be sold. The manager also determines which colors and fixtures will best compliment the store's image and merchandise. You should be able to work with space, light, and movement. An understanding of or background in architecture and/or interior design is helpful. It's also useful to have working knowledge of carpentry and construction to help in the design of the store fixtures.

Textile designer

From plaids to florals, every textile for the home or for personal apparel must be designed and printed, knitted, or woven. This includes textiles for garments, household items, carpets, and fabric wallcoverings. The designs are usually commercially produced, so detailed knowledge of mass production and manufacture is needed. Designers work in close conjunction with these manufacturers and fashion designers, so knowledge of the uses of inks, dyes, and yarns is necessary. Textile designers usually develop products by eye or with the aid of a computer. They do sketches of several design concepts, which they present for a final selection to a client, an art or design director, or a product development team. Many designers are self-employed and sell their work through studios, agents, or by direct sales. A love of fabric, a creative flair for its uses, and knowledge of the way a fabric can hang on a person or window and its overall usefulness is imperative in this profession. Creativity and originality are a must. Formal training at art school is necessary, and a study of the history of design is useful. You need to keep abreast of current trends and have the potential to visualize future ones.

Toy designer

Designing a new toy is a creative science. It also requires extreme imagination and, more often than not, technical skills. A toy designer must know something about the proper use of materials in relation to safety, durability, and ease of maintenance, as well as the technical indications of manufacturing the toy, including cost to the manufacturer. The designer should be able to work with experts in the field of child psychology and be knowledgeable about the levels of skill development in children at specific ages. In addition, you must be able to use graphic design, type, mechanical drawing, and color effectively. A sensitivity to color is also useful.

TV promotions writer

Television stations promote themselves all the time. Their promotions department will come up with ways to make the station more visible to the public with on-air competitions, public appearances by its celebrity presenters, community initiatives, and more. The main focus is to create, write, and produce the station's news, entertainment, community, and PSA on-air promotional messages to attract audiences. This includes, but is not limited to, gathering information, graphics, audio, video, logos, scripts, as well as writing and producing radio spots, public service announcements, and print advertisement for outside media. You must be able to juggle multiple projects at a time and work under extreme deadlines and pressure. You'll also need to have the drive and ambition to push the creative envelope and the talent to write killer promos. A bachelor's degree in journalism, advertising, or marketing is required.

Video game designer

Great computer skills matched with highly visual creativity puts you in position for this quickly expanding market. There are video games out there for every taste—sports, action, betting, adventure, strategy, and education—and the companies making them are keen to stay on top of the market. Games are made for personal computers, consoles, arcades, and the Internet. Games are on Web sites, electronic organizers, and even cell phones. Designing video games requires passion and creativity as well as serious skills. In every development studio, the people who make video games comprise four main teams: design, artistic, programming, and testing. The design team writes the game concept, character interactions, and game-play elements. The artistic team creates images and composes music and sound. The programming team plans and codes software. And the testing team finds errors in the game before it is published. Designers work with artists, programmers, and musicians throughout development. Aside from understanding complex computer programming and software design, designers need to have the imagination to come up with new innovations and cutting-edge ideas. The most common degree concentrations are English, art, and computer science.

Visual merchandisers

People generally won't buy something unless they like the look of it, and arranging merchandise in a store or shop window is a big part of attracting a shopper's interest. A visual merchandiser helps generate product interest by designing and putting together visually stimulating displays. They may decide to decorate the merchandise with dramatic props, color, or lighting in order to catch the consumer's eye. They are not only artists but craftspeople and may also be skilled in carpentry, painting, and the electrical wiring used to create the desired effects.

Voiceover artist

Trained voiceover artists, or voice actors, are used to do radio and TV commercials, promotions, documentaries, film narrations, cartoon voices, foreign film dubbing, and much more. It's well-paid work, especially considering the short amount of time the jobs usually entail. However, it's a very competitive industry, with even big-name actors subscribing to work in the field. However, advertising agencies typically listen to hundreds of voices in search of the one that most perfectly fits what they're trying to convey, so there's always a chance you may fit the bill, particularly if you have a unique voice or accent.

Wardrobe stylist

By selecting currently available merchandise, wardrobe stylists dress the actors in movie, television, and stage productions in anything from a sitcom such as *Friends* to a magazine format show like *Entertainment Tonight.* The job of a stylist consists of keeping up with the trends and knowing the way certain types of people look and dress in order to keep them in character for their part. They should enjoy shopping and be well versed in the different styles of fashion designers and high-street stores. It used to be considered a fundamental, necessary job rather than a creative one, but now, since some actors on TV start trends rather than follow them, wardrobe designers are becoming hailed as fashion mavens. This is a highly competitive career field that requires flexibility, creativity, and strong visual sense. Stylists generally start by working for magazines or catalogs before moving into TV or theater. A good start is to contact magazines to inquire about internships. You need to generate experience and add shoots that you have worked on in order to build up a portfolio to show to prospective clients. Remember that styling incorporates many specialties within entertainment, so make connections with photographers, makeup artists, and models. A stylist should be easy to deal with in order to get repeat work and further recommendations.

Web designer

Most companies, large and small, now have a presence on the Web, and as such, Web design is a hugely growing area. Web designers create the look, feel, and navigation for Web sites using HTML programming, which is the basic computer language for creating Web pages, as well as JAVA and a number of computer graphics programs.

New technologies, techniques, and design standards are constantly being developed, and there is an ever-increasing demand for more information, more exciting Web page designs, and increased functionality. Whether you work as part of a Web design team, within a company, or as an independent contractor, you'll need to be detail oriented, proficient at your job, and in possession of good people skills, imagination, and mastery of the design tools.

Summary

Taking the time to sit down and think about your personality and career path is time well spent. You may uncover career ideas you had never thought about before. Be realistic, too. If you prefer working alone, don't turn your artistic talents to more social jobs, like makeup artist. There is the perfect niche for your talents and skills. It's up to you to unearth it.

Tips to remember:

- Within every personality type, there are many different possible paths to choose.
- Being honest about your likes and capabilities will help you find the right one.
- Keep abreast of industry development and changes. Web designers barely existed a decade ago, so keep up with trends to see where your career could ultimately grow.

Chapter 11

Straight from the Horse's Mouth:
Advice from Those Who Have Followed
Their Heart and Their Art

Who knows better than those who have been there and done that? Some of these people are well known, but most are just regular folk who, through determination and courage, have made their personal dream happen. Here's their advice to anyone on the brink of unleashing their true ambition.

"I started designing wedding gowns about eighteen years ago by designing my own gown for my wedding. Everything I saw was more embellished than what I wanted, so I did my own. Afterwards I was convinced there were more brides like me, so I started my business. I got my big break in 1990 when I showed my first wholesale collection to Hedda Schachter, then owner of Kleinfeld. She purchased it on the spot for the store. My business took off after that. Now my designs have made regular appearances on Hollywood's red carpets, adorning such stars as Julia Roberts, Halle Berry, Salma Hayek, Lucy Liu, Heather Graham, Lynn Redgrave, and many others. In addition to my Madison Avenue boutique, my bridal and evening designs are found nationwide at the finest boutiques and specialty retailers, such as Bergdorf Goodman, Saks Fifth Avenue, and Neiman Marcus stores. My advice is, once you decide what you want to do, and

it's something that you really believe in, go for it, and don't stop
until you get it."

—*Amsale Aberra, bridal designer*

"Thoughts are things; they have tremendous power. Thoughts
of doubt and fear are pathways to failure. When you conquer negative attitudes of doubt and fear, you conquer failure. Thoughts crys-
tallize into habit and habit, solidifies into circumstances."

—*Bryan Adams, singer/songwriter*

"Eighty percent of success is showing up."

—*Woody Allen, actor, director*

"By age eleven, I aspired to become a writer. I did investigative
and white-collar crime reporting, and then the small business column at *The Los Angeles Times*. It was picked up for syndication and
today reaches 8 million readers. A radio show and several books on
entrepreneurship followed before I formed my own production company. Hard work does equal success. There is no magic formula; 90
percent of it is working day and night and being relentless."

—*Jane Applegate, author and founder,*
Small Business Television Network

"I worked for the same exhibition display company for sixteen
years. The company had been new and exciting at first, but it had
since become so big, I felt taken for granted. It was the most difficult
decision of my life, but I left with no contacts at all and set up a new
company with my friend Philip. We're now getting lots of work for
great people designing museum interiors, including the HMS *Belfast*
on the River Thames in London. When work stops being fun, it's
time to make a move. Don't hang on; you've got to be brave."

—*Karen Balme, exhibit designer*

"My love affair with makeup started when I first discovered my mother's collection of cosmetics. My mom always intrigued and inspired me with her glamour and her beauty rituals. I went on to learn the art of theatrical makeup at Emerson College in Boston, then headed for New York City to work as a professional makeup artist. It wasn't long before I became frustrated by the lack of flattering makeup on the market for certain skin tones. In 1991, I debuted a line of cosmetics—just ten brown-based lipsticks—at Bergdorf Goodman in New York City. The line gained a strong following first among beauty insiders, then women everywhere. Today, Bobbi Brown Cosmetics can be found throughout North America, Europe, and Asia. My mantra: Keep it simple, real, and approachable."

—*Bobbi Brown, founder and CEO of Bobbi Brown Cosmetics*

"I've always explored different creative fields. I took a degree in art in my native Canada, I've taught photography, and I've taken classes to learn how to make lithographs. But the class that captured my imagination most was learning to make stained glass. Meanwhile, I brought up two sons alone after my divorce, so I worked as a community nurse to support them until they both left home. Now I work part-time as a lecturer training nurses and run a business designing, making, and fitting stained glass panels. I have a workshop in my backyard, and I get a steady flow of work. Do only the jobs that you want to do. Design things that are fun and challenging, but don't make your life difficult by making it too fancy."

—*Jennie Burgen, creator of stained glass windows*

"I started Callaway at the age of twenty-five. It's a family entertainment company specializing in publishing, animation for film and television, and children's lifestyle product design—recent projects include Madonna's children's books and the Miss Spider computer-animated television series. I had three valuable assets: ignorance, poverty, and inexperience. These motivated me to learn more, work harder, and think more creatively in order to succeed. The only invaluable asset I had—and have—are relationships. The most important lesson I've learned in twenty-five years of being an entrepreneur is to treat everyone you meet in business—customers, partners, employees, and adversaries—as generously as you possibly can. You can never overestimate how much you may need them or how much they may help you when you least expect it."

—*Nicholas Callaway, CEO of Callaway Arts & Entertainment*

"Talent alone won't make you a success. Neither will being in the right place at the right time, unless you are ready. The most important question is: 'Are you ready?'"

—*Johnny Carson, comedian, TV presenter*

"I don't know the key to success, but the key to failure is trying to please everybody."

—*Bill Cosby, actor*

"A person is a success if they get up in the morning and get to bed at night and in between does what he wants to do."

—*Bob Dylan, singer/songwriter*

"The only thing that separates successful people from the ones who aren't is the willingness to work very, very hard."

—*Helen Gurley Brown, founder of* Cosmopolitan *magazine*

"I applied to McDonald's, but didn't get the job. In 1970, I tried standup comedy and was discovered by singer Nancy Wilson. I later toured, opening for twenty major headliners including Patti LaBelle, Aretha Franklin, Tina Turner, and Stevie Wonder. On January 3, 1989, *The Arsenio Hall Show* made its debut. During a successful five-year run, it provided a forum for cutting-edge comedy, politics, and the television debut of Mariah Carey, Snoop Doggy

Dogg, Boyz II Men, and countless others. For people trying to make it out there, do what you do as often as you can. Ignore the financial compensation. The money will come."

—Arsenio Hall, actor, comedian, and producer

"As a child, I developed a sense of the significant bond between people and animals. This emotional connection became fully realized when I began taking riding lessons as a young adult. Soon after, I bought a horse and this love affair has continued to grow and evolve. I love to paint, and I began creating stylized paintings of horses in acrylic. I aim to capture the horses' energy, incredible strength, gentleness, and independence of spirit and paint images that provide a unique perspective on nature. I work out of my home studio in central New Jersey, and I've been able to build up a collection of work that's been included at significant exhibitions at Les Malamut Gallery and the Renee Foosaner Art Gallery. I think you need to find something that moves you and that inspires your creativity. My art is a reflection of my deep compassion and admiration for the horse and other wildlife."

—Lin Salerno, food research and development

"I was born and grew up in Dublin, Ireland. My parents were working-class people, and in those days in Ireland being poor meant being *really* poor. Often I would draw on the cardboard from discarded boxes that I got from the local grocery store. As I grew up, I never lost my passion for art, and when I started working, I was able to buy oil paints. I was a typical working-class Dubliner, and though my passion was art, I had to work at a regular job to support my family. Painting did help me escape from the monotony of my regular job, though, and whenever I worked on a painting, I was transported to another world and found peace and contentment. I came to the United States in 1978 with my wife and our eleven-month-old daughter, and my life really changed. I concentrated on making a decent living and twenty-five years later, although still not earning a living as a professional artist, I am happy with what I have accomplished career-wise. I love backpacking and hiking, so about five years ago I bought a camera to enable me to take photos of the wonderful things I saw around me in nature. Little did I know it would turn into a bigger passion than my love of painting. Digital photography has opened up a whole new world of creativity, and I now spend many happy hours taking photos and manipulating them on the computer. The creative possibilities seem to be endless in this medium, and I get more excited with it as time goes on. I have been fortunate enough to have had one exhibition of my work and have sold some of my photos on the Internet. I still work long hours at my regular job but over time I plan to open up a home studio and also actively pursue selling my work via the Internet. It's important to keep your ambitions going. That lifelong dream of earning a living as a creative artist is still alive in me and stronger than ever, and continues to energize my life."

—*Martin Kavanagh, print technician*

"If you have it in you, it will come out someday. Meanwhile, keep writing. That's the trick, if there is one."

—*Stephen King, author*

"I wanted to be a makeup artist, so I took a course in hairdressing and makeup, but it was eighteen months before I landed my first magazine job. I survived by working as a beauty consultant in a large store on the weekends and taking my portfolio to art directors and photographers during the week. I've gone on to work on *Arena*, *Elle*, *Tatler*, and Spanish and German editions of *Vogue*—all done without an agent. The money's not amazing, but I'm comfortable and don't have work every day. I have fun and meet some great people. My advice is to go to the library and read about different careers first. Before you start, talk to different makeup artists, or ask to go out with them and see what they do. There are so many fields in makeup—fashion, TV, film, even prosthetics. You need to find out which one you want to do."

—Michelle Marsh, freelance makeup artist

"I work as the art director of a glossy magazine, but my real love is music. I'm a singer-songwriter and guitarist. First I was with a Celtic band called The Barleycorns, which became quite successful. Then I formed Raving Noah, and we play a wider variety of styles. I also ran a fanzine at night, too, with a fellow band member. My advice to aspiring musicians is—don't give up your day job! Seriously, not until you really have to. It's the day job that allows you to put the money you make back into the band. Don't waste what little time you have in the evening to get things done either. Treat your band like a business. When you're not writing, rehearsing, recording, or gigging, you should be busy promoting yourself. Besides making tons of phone calls to labels, agents, promoters, and radio stations, making posters, and maintaining a Web site and a mailing list, that also means talking your band up at bars, parties, and family gatherings! There's a way to do it without making yourself a pariah. I would also say if you're getting a positive response, work even harder. If you're doing all you can and the audiences aren't growing and the gigs aren't coming your way, rethink your direction. It may mean starting all over again with a different sound or a different band. If things are going well, take some long weekends off work to tour outside your area. Hook up with the college or festival circuit and book a supporting gig while you're in town. Don't forget to alert the local media. Sometimes a visiting band is a bigger deal than a hometown one."

—Andrew Ogilvie, art director, musician

"If you're climbing the ladder of life, you go rung by rung, one step at a time. Don't look too far up; set your goals high, but take one step at a time. Sometimes you don't think you're progressing until you step back and see how high you've really gone."

—*Donny Osmond, singer, TV personality*

"If you really want to do it, you will do it. You will find the time. And it might not be much time, but you'll make it. Obviously if you have homework or other activities, you're not going to have huge amounts of time, but if you really want to, you'll do it. You have to resign yourself to wasting lots of trees before you write anything really good. That's just how it is. It's like learning an instrument. You've got to be prepared for hitting wrong notes occasionally, or quite a lot. That's just part of the learning process. And read a lot. Reading a lot really helps. Read anything you can get your hands on."

—*J.K. Rowling, author of the Harry Potter books*

"As a former college basketball player, I find team sports has helped me approach the team working atmosphere. I really value self-starters and people who are motivated. Put in your dues. Volunteer. Meet people. There are ways to break in. You really are in control of your own career. You can't wait for other people to guide you. You have to take the initiative."

—*Anucha Browne Sanders, senior vice president, Marketing and Business Operations, New York Knicks*

"I make brooches and earrings from plastic and wholesale to galleries and craft shops. To be successful, you must take your product around to different places. Don't rely on craft markets, which can be tedious and don't make much money. Wholesale is the way to go. If your product is different, priced right, and of a good enough quality, the craft shops and galleries will buy it."

—*Cara Sandys, jewelry maker*

"I grew up writing letters and stories. I was an entrepreneur as a child, writing, selling my used children's books, lemonade, whatever. As an adult, I become a journalist and writer. I have been on over 100 TV/radio shows and my work has appeared in magazines and newspapers while my books have been published in over twenty languages around the world. Early on, I followed the motto of a rags-to-riches man who told me 'I was too stupid to know any better,' and that's how I made it. Nothing was ever impossible. There were always other routes one could take or circumvent."

—Jacqueline Simenauer, author and columnist

"It is uncomfortable doing something that's risky. But so what? Do you want to stagnate and just be comfortable?"

—Barbra Streisand, singer, actress, director

"About fifteen years ago, after rescuing an injured pigeon, I learned about wildlife rehabilitation. After apprenticing for two years with a wildlife rehabilitator, I became New Jersey licensed and funded my hobby through my job in the information technology field. I also began to foster dogs and cats for rescue groups, volunteer at the local shelter by walking dogs, and sometimes rescue animals. Last year, after losing my job, rather than go back into the corporate world, I created a job for myself. I started All About Animals— which does pet sitting, dog walking, dog behavior modification, and coexistence with wildlife. My advice is to not do what you have to, but to do what you choose to."

—Renee Thomaier, animal rights activist

"I've worked as a motoring journalist for twenty years, and have been freelance for more than half that time. I fell into journalism entirely by accident having answered an advertisement for an office junior. I discovered I loved both writing and cars. The decision to go freelance wasn't hard because I was unhappy in the all-male environment and felt restricted writing in just one style for one magazine. I began building up my freelance work before leaving my job, writing to magazines and newspapers, sending samples with a couple of carefully targeted ideas. In order to make it freelance, it's vital to read plenty of magazines and newspapers to see what everyone else is doing, and think of ideas that pick up on what's happening in the news."

—Liz Turner, freelance journalist

"I was age sixty-two before I took up botanical illustration seriously, although I had always enjoyed painting and drawing my few free moments in between working as a librarian and bringing up two daughters. It began almost by accident when I saw an exhibition of botanical illustration while attending a gardening course. It rocked me back—I stood and looked at it, this beautiful work showing how the plant grows, scientific but a work of art, too. I took a course with Christabel King, an illustrator for the world-famous Kew Gardens in London. It was very hard, but she taught me how to look and really see how the plants were constructed. From there, I researched the subject at the library, found out who the top names were, and attended courses where they teach. Now, at seventy-five, I exhibit and sell my work. My advice—seek out the best teachers and be prepared to work hard."

—Rosamund Turner, botanical illustrator

"I believe the best way to achieve success is to be passionate about what you do. When I was a young boy, I often helped my father fix things in our house in Miami. That's how I discovered that I had a passion for building. After spending two years in Panama working for the Peace Corp and two years in Stuttgart, Germany, working as an editor for the translation bureau and as a stagehand at the state theater, I decided to pursue a career where my passion burned the most—architecture. I enrolled at the Boston

Architectural Center, a cooperative studies program that allowed me to start a contracting company at the same time. I took a great interest in fixing up old houses. One of the first homes I fixed was the subject of a *Boston Globe* article. It was this article that led to me being discovered and launching a lasting career in television— twenty-five years this September, 2004."

—*Bob Vila, home-improvement expert, author, executive producer and host of* Home Again

"I came to New York from Cuba in 1961 at the age of twenty-five. I had a business degree and I was an accountant. In Cuba, my family ran a wholesale and retail business, purchasing merchandise from the United States, selling it in their store, and distributing to other stores throughout the country. My brother got work in a hardware store in Greenwich Village and knew some suppliers. They extended us six months' credit, so we opened a small hardware store. We ordered the right merchandise, treated customers well, and built up a strong clientele. The store has kept growing and now is three storefronts throughout Manhattan. We now sell a variety of goods from the proverbial nuts and bolts of hardware supplies, to dazzling crystal finials imported from France, to the prettiest bed linens from around the world. Customer service is always at the forefront. If we don't have what customers ask for, we order it, and not just the most popular items. We want to keep every individual customer satisfied. You must never give up. When you want to throw in the towel, don't. Eventually it will be tomorrow, and if you believe in what you are doing and treat customers well, you will do well. We bend over backwards for customers, and they appreciate it."

—*Natan Wekselbaum, founder and owner of* Gracious Home *stores*

"During the mid-'70s, when New York's tourism industry had sunk to an all-time low, I engineered the "I Love New York" campaign, which ultimately helped to draw billions of dollars in tourism to the city. Today, I run my own Manhattan-based PR consulting firm, and clients have included Diana Ross, Carly Simon, and Kevin Costner. You have to realize you don't make a lot of money in this field. You need to be strongly independent and able to maintain your integrity."

—Bobby Zarem, publicity agent

Resources

The first part of this section lists organizations, Web sites, and publications that may be helpful to you in managing your career and your passion, no matter what field you are interested in working in. The second part, Resources by Field, is an alphabetical list of resources in different career areas.

General Resources

Business Coaching

The International Coach Federation
www.coachfederation.org
Professional coaches provide an ongoing partnership designed to help clients produce fulfilling results in their personal and professional lives.

Catalogs

www.catalogage.com
Catalog design, production and creative services agency.

www.catalogcity.com
An online catalog shopping super site, which sells a range of products from top-brand catalogs.

www.shop.com
A premiere catalog-shopping site on the Internet, with over 7 million products from more than 500 merchants. Has developed partnerships with the largest Web portals, affinity sites, and *Fortune* 500 companies, as well as major merchants in the mail order, online catalog, and retail businesses.

Distance Education

United States Distance Learning Association
www.usdla.org
The United States Distance Learning Association is a 501(c)(3) non-profit association formed in 1987 and located in Boston, Massachusetts. USDLA promotes the development and application of distance learning for education and training and serves the needs of the distance learning community by providing advocacy, information, networking, and opportunity.

The Department of Education
www.ed.gov

Kaplan College
www.kaplancollege.edu

University of Phoenix
www.universityofphoenixonline.com

Franchising

International Franchise Association
www.franchise.org
Membership organization of franchisers, franchisees, and suppliers. Web site is dedicated to providing members and guests with a one-stop shopping experience for franchise information.

Trade magazines

Franchising World
www.franchise.org

Books

Franchising for Dummies co-authored by Dave Thomas, the founder of Wendy's (For Dummies)

Franchising: A Pathway to Wealth Creation by Bob Rosenberg and Steven Spinella (Pearson Education)

Interactive Advertising

Association for Interactive Media
www.aaf.org
The largest trade association in the world devoted to helping companies that use the Internet and interactive media to reach their respective marketplaces with maximum effectiveness. Serves diverse corporate interests from e-mail marketing, e-tailing, online marketing, content provision, e-commerce, market research, broadband access, and the rollout of interactive television.

Association of National Advertisers, Inc.
www.ana.net
Trade association dedicated exclusively to marketing and brand building. ANA serves the needs of its members by providing marketing and advertising industry leadership in traditional and e-marketing, legislative leadership, information resources, professional development, and industry-wide networking.

Interactive Advertising Bureau
www.iab.net
Interactive advertising association. Its activities include evaluating and recommending guidelines and best practices, fielding research to document the effectiveness of interactive media, and educating the advertising industry about the use of interactive advertising and marketing.

Internships

www.internships.com
Large database of internships and job postings.

www.wetfeet.com
The WetFeet Network provides information on companies, careers, and industries that job seekers use throughout their careers to make smarter career decisions. WetFeet also offers job seekers expert advice, newsletters, salary benchmarking tools, and discussion boards on everything from negotiating a raise to writing better cover letters.

Books:

Internship Success by Marianne Ehrlich Greene (Career Horizons)
America's Top Internships and *The Internship Bible* by Mark Oldman and Samer Hamadeh (Random House)

Mentoring

The National Mentoring Partnership
www.mentoring.org
Nonprofit organization, which structures customized mentoring programs for students ages eight through eighteen throughout school districts, with volunteers from corporations.

America's Promise
www.americaspromise.org
The mission of America's Promise is to mobilize people from every sector of American life to build the character and competence of youth by fulfilling the Five Promises declared at the Presidents' Summit for America's Future: caring adults (parents, mentors, tutors, and coaches); safe places with structured activities during nonschool hours; a healthy start; marketable skills through effective education; and opportunities for all young people to serve.

Microlending

Count Me In

www.count-me-in.org
The first online microlender, Count Me In uses a unique women-friendly credit scoring system to make loans of $500 to $10,000 available to women across the United States who have nowhere to turn for that all-important first business loan.

Small Business Association Micro Lenders

www.sbaonline.sba.gov/financing/sbaloan/microloans.html
Program provides very small loans to start-up, newly established, or growing small business concerns.

Networking/Office Politics

Books

Nonstop Networking: How to Improve Your Life, Luck, and Career by Andrea Nierenberg (Capital Books)

Work Would Be Great if It Weren't for the People by Ronna Lichtenberg (Hyperion)

Networlding: Building Relationships and Opportunities for Success by Melissa Giovagnoli and Jocelyn Carter-Miller (Jossey-Bass)

Public Relations

www.prweb.com
Offers free online press release distribution services. Claims to be the largest newswire catering to small- and medium-sized companies and organizations and one of the largest online press release newswires.

www.publicityhound.com
Free articles on how to catch the attention of frazzled news directors, busy reporters, and grumpy editors.

Small Business

Small Business Administration
www.sba.gov
Mission is to maintain and strengthen the nation's economy by aiding, counseling, assisting, and protecting the interests of small businesses and by helping families and businesses recover from national disasters.

SEEDCO
www.seedco.org
Provides financial and technical assistance and management support for the community-building efforts of nonprofit organizations and small businesses in targeted disadvantaged communities throughout the United States.

The Service Corps of Retired Executives
www.score.org
Nonprofit association dedicated to providing entrepreneurs with free, confidential face-to-face, and e-mail business counseling.

Axxess Business Centers
www.abcbizhelp.net
For-profit consulting firm. Helps nation's small business owners and millions of other aspiring entrepreneurs to achieve their corporate best by providing them with fast, friendly, and affordable consulting through a nationwide chain of walk-in centers conveniently located in major metropolitan markets.

American Institute of Small Business
(952) 545-7001

Trade Shows

Trade Show News Network
www.tsnn.com
Leading online resource for the twenty-second largest industry in the world—the trade show and exhibition industry. TSNN owns and operates the most widely consulted database on the Internet for the trade show industry, containing data on more than 15,000 trade shows and conferences, and through a strategic partnership, more than 30,000 seminars.

Trend Forecasting

Faith Popcorn's Brain Reserve
www.faithpopcorn.com
(212) 772-7778

Trends Research Institute® Inc.
P.O. Box 660
Rhinebeck, NY 12572-0660

The Institute for the Future
www.iftf.org
Nonprofit research group focused on providing strategic insights into business strategy, product design processes, and new business development.

Venture Capital

www.moneyhunter.com
Downloadable business plan templates.

Let's Talk Business Network
www.ltbn.com
Online, entrepreneurial support community.

Web Business

Books

Making Money with Your Computer at Home by Paul and Sarah Edwards (Tarcher/Putnam)

Directory of Medical Management Software by Gary Knox (Resource Books, California)

The Fine Art of Technical Writing by Carol Rosenblum Perry (Blue Heron Publishing)

The Everything® Online Business Book by Rob Liflander (Adams Media)

Work/Life

Alliance of Work/Life Professionals
www.awlp.org
Provides professional membership services to individuals and organizations that are focused on creating healthy work environments that value people and support personal life and family issues.

The Center for Work and the Family
www.centerforworkandfamily.com
Worksite-based seminars developed to increase understanding of work/life stress, improve communication and coping skills, teach problem solving, and further a dialogue about work/life issues between employees and employers.

Couple Biz
www.couplebiz.com
Husband-wife psychologist team consulting to business couples.

Workspace Organization

The National Association of Professional Organizers
www.napo.net
Nonprofit educational association whose members include organizing consultants, speakers, trainers, authors, and manufacturers of organizing products.

Books

Organize Your Office! Simple Routines for Managing Your Workspace by Ronni Eisenberg (Hyperion)

Workaholism

Workaholics Anonymous
www.workaholics-anonymous.org
Has nationwide chapters and regular meetings.

Resources by Field

Album Cover Design

The Album Cover Network
www.albumcovers.net/fr_frameset.asp
This site is dedicated to the celebration of the art of the 12x12-inch vinyl record jacket. Inside you will find vinyl record jackets of popular rock music from the 1960s on up. It also has links to musician, artist/designer, and other types of sites that have vinyl record images.

Alternative Healing

Alternative Medicine Foundation
www.amfoundation.org
Nonprofit organization, founded in March 1998, to provide responsible and reliable information about alternative medicine to the public and health professionals.

Alternative Therapies in Health and Medicine
www.alternative-therapies.com
Forum for sharing information concerning the practical use of alternative therapies in preventing and treating disease, healing illness, and promoting health.

American Massage Therapy Association
www.amtamassage.org
Represents more than 47,000 massage therapists in twenty-seven countries. Works to establish massage therapy as integral to the maintenance of good health and complementary to other therapeutic processes, and to advance the profession through ethics and standards, certification, school accreditation, continuing education, professional publications, legislative efforts, public education, and professional development of members.

American Organization for Bodywork Therapies of Asia
www.aobta.org
National not-for-profit professional association of practitioners of Bodywork Therapies of Asia.

The National Certification Commission for Acupuncture and Oriental Medicine (NCCAOM)
www.nccaom.org
Nonprofit organization. Its mission is to establish, assess, and promote recognized standards of competence and safety in acupuncture and Oriental medicine for the protection and benefit of the public.

American Holistic Nurses Association
www.ahna.org
Nonprofit educational organization whose membership is open to nurses and other individuals interested in holistically-oriented health care practices throughout the United States and the world. AHNA supports the education of nurses, allied health practitioners, and the general public on health-related issues.

Trade Magazines

Massage Therapy Journal
www.amtamassage.org

Massage
www.massagemag.com

Animation

Animation World Network
www.awn.com
The largest animation-related publishing group on the Internet, providing readers from more than 145 countries with a wide range of interesting, relevant, and helpful information pertaining to all aspects of animation. Covering areas as diverse as animator profiles, independent film distribution, commercial studio activities, CGI, and other animation technologies, as well as in-depth coverage of current events in all fields of animation.

Trade Magazines

Animation Journal
www.animationjournal.com
Founded in 1991, *Animation Journal* is the only peer-reviewed scholarly journal devoted to animation history and theory. Its content reflects the diversity of animation's production techniques and national origins.

Antiques/Restoration

Association of Restorers, Inc.
www.assoc-restorers.com
(315) 733-1952
Mission is to raise the awareness of choices to conserve, refurbish, or restore historical works of art, household furnishings, and architectural constructions. Through education and networking, the best method will be selected to enhance, stabilize, and return a piece to its original beauty, use, or condition.

Trade Magazines

Art & Antiques
www.artandantiques.net

Books

Buying and Selling Antiques by Don Cline and Sara Pitzer (Storey Books)

Art/Music Therapy

Art Therapy Grad Schools
www.gradschools.com/listings/east/art_therapy_east.html

American Art Therapy Association, Inc.
www.arttherapy.org
An organization of professionals dedicated to the belief that the creative process involved in the making of art is healing and life-enhancing.

Music Therapy Link
http://members.aol.com/kathysl/index.html
This site was created as a place to gather information, help open the lines of communication and networking, and educate the public about the field of music therapy.

Art As a Healing Force
www.artashealing.org
This site concentrates on making art to heal, on the power of the creative process of art as a healing force.

Bed and Breakfasts

Professional Association of Innkeepers International
www.paii.org
Claims to be the world's largest trade association supporting innkeepers.

Comic Books

Ask Art
http://askart.com/interest/topcartoon.asp
Listing of various comic book artists and Web sites dedicated to their work.

Kubert School of Cartoon and Graphic Art
www.kubertsworld.com
The school is located in Dover, New Jersey, and is dedicated to aspiring cartoonists who are dedicated to becoming professionals in cartooning, comic book, and the general field of commercial art. In addition to the major in cartoon graphics, the school also offers a major in cinematic animation.

www.comicbookresources.com
The ultimate online resource for comic book enthusiasts.

www.digitalwebbing.com
The comic book creator's newspage. Daily news about your favorite comic book and comic strip Web sites. Also a database of Web sites, comic book news, talent search classifieds, and interviews.

National Cartoonists Society
www.reuben.org
World's largest and most prestigious organization of professional cartoonists.

Graphic Artists Guild
www.gag.org
National union of illustrators, designers, Web creators, production artists, surface designers, and other creatives who have come together to pursue common goals, share their experience, raise industry standards, and improve the ability of visual creators to achieve satisfying and rewarding careers.

Association of American Editorial Cartoonists
http://info.detnews.com/aaec
Membership includes full-time editorial cartoonists, student cartoonists, and others with a professional interest in cartooning.

Comic Con
www.comicon.com
Online comic book convention of global proportions. Features message boards, chat rooms, news and commentary, and easy access to the sites of many Kubert School alumni.

Books
Comics and Sequential Art by Will Eisner (Poorhouse Press)

Understanding Comics; The Invisible Art by Scott McCloud (Perennial Currents)

Children of the Yellow Kid: The Evolution of the American Comic Strip by Robert C. Harvey, Richard V. West, and Brian Walker (U of Washington Press)

Cosmetology

Beauty & Barber Supply Institute (BBSI)
www.bbsi.org

American Board of Certified Haircolorists (ABCH)
28132 Western Avenue
San Pedro, CA 90732
(310) 547-0814; FAX (310) 547-3743

National Alliance of Salon Professionals (NASP)
194 Talquin Hideaway Road
Quincy, FL 32351
(850) 875-9707; (888) 385-3330

The Salon Association (TSA)
www.salons.org

Nails Industry Association (NIA)
2512 Artesia Blvd.
Redondo Beach, CA 90278
(310) 376-9438; (800) 846-2457
FAX (310) 376-9043

Costume Design

Costume Society of America
www.costumesocietyamerica.com
Publishes educational journal *Dress.*

National Costumers Association
www.costumers.org
U.S.–based group supporting the costuming industry. Officers and board of directors, mission statement, events schedule, image gallery from past competitions, scholarships, list of members, and membership form.

Culinary Arts

Culinary Institute of America
www.ciachef.edu

Le Cordon Bleu
www.lecordonbleuschoolsusa.com
Personal Chef Association
www.personalchef.com

American Culinary Federation
www.acfchefs.org

Online Magazines

www.gourmet.com

www.bonappetit.com

Dance Education

National Dance Education Organization

www.ndeo.org

An autonomous nonprofit organization dedicated to promoting standards of excellence in dance education by providing the dance artist and the dance educator with a network of resources and support, a base for advocacy, and access to programs and projects that focus on the importance of dance in the human experience.

American Alliance for Health, Physical Education, Recreation and Dance

www.aahperd.org

Daycare

Nation's Network of Child Care Resource & Referral Services

www.naccrra.com

National network of more than 850 child-care resource and referral centers (CCR&Rs) located in every state and most communities across the United States. CCR&R centers help families, child-care providers, and communities find, provide, and plan for affordable, quality childcare.

Day Care Council of America

5730 Market Street

Oakland, CA 94608

Ergonomics

Human Factors and Ergonomics Society
www.hfes.org
Furthers consideration of knowledge about the assignment of appropriate functions for humans and machines, whether people serve as operators, maintainers, or users in the system.

Occupational Safety and Health Administration (OSHA)
www.osha.gov
Federal and state governments working in partnership with the more than 100 million working men and women and their six and a half million employers who are covered by the Occupational Safety and Health Act of 1970.

Degree Programs:

Occupational and Industrial Orthopedic Center, Hospital for Joint Diseases at New York University
301 E 17th St.
New York, NY
(212) 598-6000
www.hjd.org

Event Planning

International Society of Meeting Planners
www.iami.org
Providing professional recognition and a method to easily network with recognized professionals in the meeting planning industry.

Trade Magazines:

Special Events
Biz Buzz

Event Marketer
Successful Meetings

Feng Shui

International Feng Shui Guild
www.fengshuiguild.com
Claims to be a benevolent oasis for all aspects and for all schools of feng shui, serving professional practitioners as well as anyone interested in this ancient art of placement. Dedicated to advancing the practice, teaching, and use of feng shui globally.

Feng Shui Society
www.fengshuisociety.org.uk
Nonprofit organization based in the United Kingdom, with links throughout the world, committed to improving the quality and integrity of feng shui practice.

Floral Design

American Institute of Floral Designers
www.aifd.org
Information on floral design and professional careers in floral designing.

Association of Specialty Cut Flower Growers
www.ascfg.org
Trade association for commercial cut flower growers.

Trade Magazines

Floral & Nursery Times
P.O. Box 8470, Northfield, IL 60093;
(847) 784-9797
The floral industry's international news magazine with news, features, and moneymaking ideas using four-color photos and articles by AIFD and other well-known designers.

Graphic Design

American Institute of Graphic Arts (AIGA)
www.aiga.org
The oldest and largest membership association for professionals engaged in the discipline, practice, and culture of designing. Supports the interests of professionals, educators, and students who are engaged in the process of designing, regardless of where they are in the arc of their careers.

Art Directors Club
www.adcglobal.org
An international not-for-profit organization of leading creatives in advertising, graphic design, interactive media, broadcast design, typography, packaging, environmental design, photography, illustration, and related disciplines.

Art Years
www.artyears.com
Community portal offering tips and resources for graphic designers.

Handcrafts

National Crafts Association
www.craftassoc.com

Knitting Guild Association
www.tkga.com

www.craftsfairguide.com
Publication for artists and craftspeople that lists and reviews arts and craft fairs in California, Oregon, Washington, Nevada, and Arizona. It reviews approximately 1,000 arts and craft fairs occurring throughout the West.

Magazines

American Woodworker
Jo-Ann Magazine
Doll Crafter
Knit It!

Horticulture

Royal Horticulture Society
www.rhs.org.uk
Britain's largest gardening charity, committed to being the leading organization demonstrating excellence in horticulture and promoting gardening. Source of advice and information for all gardeners.

Imagineer

Walt Disney Imagineering/Career Information
http://disney.go.com/DisneyCareers/WhoWeAre/
Imagineering.html
1401 Flower Street
P.O. Box 25020
Glendale, CA 91221-5020

**International Association of Amusement Parks
and Attractions**
www.iaapa.org
Nonprofit organization with a membership consisting of fixed-site facilities and suppliers. The association is dedicated to the preservation and prosperity of the amusement industry worldwide.

Interior Design Resources

American Society of Interior Designers
www.asid.org

www.interiordesignjobs.com

Magazines

Interiors
Interior Design

Jewelry Making

Jewelry Designers Guild
www.jewelrydesignersguild.com
Internet community for artists creating unique jewelry made from materials as diverse as can be imagined.

Magazines

Lapidary Journal
www.lapidaryjournal.com
Claims to be the first gem and jewelry-making magazine in the world! Now more than fifty years old, it's still dedicated to the art of gems, jewelry making, beads, minerals, and more.

Books

Jewelry Design: The Artist's Reference by Elizabeth Olver (North Light Books)

Landscape Architecture

American Society of Landscape Architects
www.asla.org
National professional association for landscape architects representing 14,200 members.

American Association of Botanical Gardens and Arboreta
www.aabga.org
Association for North American public gardens and their professional staff. Publishes a monthly newsletter, the quarterly journal, *The Public Garden*, and many other publications, and sponsors six regional meetings and one national conference each year.

Council of Landscape Architectural Registration Boards
www.clarb.org
General information on registration or licensing requirements is available.

Magazine Industry

Magazine Publishers of America
www.magazine.org
The industry association for consumer magazines. Established in 1919, the MPA represents more than 240 domestic publishing companies with approximately 1,400 titles, more than 80 international companies, and more than 100 associate members.

Mural Design

Metro Murals
www.metromurals.org
Metromurals does community-based murals.

Murals Plus
www.muralsplus.com
Muralsplus.com is a community project for all muralists, faux painters, stencilers, and decorative painters.

Museums

American Association of Museums
www.aam-us.org
Represents the entire scope of museums, museum professionals, and nonpaid staff who work for and with museums. Dedicated to promoting excellence within the museum community through advocacy, professional education, information exchange, accreditation, and guidance on current professional standards of performance.

Pet Industry

American Pet Products Manufacturers Association
www.appma.org

National Dog Groomers Association of America, Inc.
www.nationaldoggroomers.com
Workshop education, National Certified Master Groomer program, newsletter (three times a year), grooming seminars, groomer insurance opportunities, job placement program, grooming contests, and much more. With 2,500 members, they are the pet grooming industry's largest pet groomer association, working to promote excellence in professional and set standards of performance.

The National Association of Pet Sitters

http://petsitters.org

A national professional trade association such as the National Association of Professional Pet Sitters provides valuable credibility, networking, and education that helps foster success. The National Association of Professional Pet Sitters became a nonprofit membership organization in 1993, after being founded in 1989, to promote excellence among pet sitters and to serve as a voice for the expanding industry.

Trade Magazines

Pet Age

www.petage.com

Pet industry's most popular trade magazine. Helps owners/managers of retail pet supply outlets succeed in today's competitive business environment.

Photography

American Society of Media Photographers

www.asmp.org

Claims to be the premier resource for community, culture, commerce, and publications relating to publication photography.

Magazines

Shutterbug

www.shutterbug.net

Provides classifieds, industry updates, product previews, test reports, tips, links, how-to projects, highlights of articles, and more.

Outdoor Photographer

www.outdoorphotographer.com

Restaurant and Food Industry

FoodNet
www.foodnet.com
Resource for food service industry professionals. Includes news, links, featured chefs, chat, and more.

Nation's Restaurant News
www.nrn.com
Up-to-the-minute foodservice industry news, trade show and events schedules, and business and franchise information.

Radio Programming

Talkers Magazine Online
www.talkers.com
Leading trade publication serving the talk radio industry in America. It has been dubbed "The Bible of Talk Radio" by *BusinessWeek* magazine.

Satellite Radio

Sirius Satellite Radio
www.sirius.com
Offers 100 streams of satellite radio: sixty-one devoted to commercial-free music, in almost every genre imaginable, and over forty streams dedicated to sports, news, and entertainment.

XM Satellite Radio
www.xmradio.com
XM is America's number one satellite radio service with more than 1.5 million subscribers today. Broadcasting live daily from studios in Washington, DC, New York City, and Nashville, Tennessee, at the Country Music Hall of Fame, XM's lineup includes more than 120 digital channels of choice from coast to coast.

Screenwriting and Film

Academy of Motion Picture Arts and Sciences

www.oscars.org

The Academy of Motion Picture Arts and Sciences is a professional honorary organization composed of more than 6,000 motion picture craftsmen and women.

American Screenwriters Association

www.asascreenwriters.com

Nonprofit organization for educational purposes, including the promotion and encouragement of the art of screenwriting. Committed to the international support and advancement of all screenwriters and individuals from around the world who are pursuing the writing of documentaries, educational films, feature films, television, and even radio and large screen format.

Association of Independent Video and Filmmakers

www.aivf.org

A national service organization for independent media. With over 5,000 members, AIVF is a vital resource for independent film and videomakers, providing programs and services.

Spa Industry

National Pool and Spa Institute

www.nspi.org

International trade association of more than 5,300 manufacturers, distributors, retailers, service companies, and builders in the pool/spa and hot tub industry.

Trade Magazines

American Spa
www.americanspamag.com

Pool and Spa Living
www.poolspaliving.com

Aqua
www.aquamagazine.com

Stationery/Greeting Card

Annual Stationery Show
www.nationalstationeryshow.com
Annual trade show and marketing event. Buyers know it as the premier market for greeting cards and social stationery, writing instruments and home office products, party ware and gift-wrap, scrapbooking and craft supplies, albums, frames, and more.

The Greeting Card Association (GCI)
www.greetingcard.org
GCA is an organization representing greeting card and stationery publishers and allied members of the industry.

Hallmark
www.hallmark.com
For employment information, click on About Hallmark and then Career Opportunities

American Greetings
http://corporate.americangreetings.com
For employment information, click on Frequent Questions and then Contact Us.

Television

National Association of Television
Programming Executives
www.natpe.org

International Association of Women
in Radio and Television
www.iawrt.org
Founded in 1951, this is a forum for personal contact and professional
development among women broadcasters worldwide.

Web Design

HTML Writers Guild
www.hwg.org
A Web design community, with over 150,000 members in more than
160 countries worldwide. In 2001 the Guild joined with the International Webmaster's Association to form IWA-HWG, the professional
association for the growth of the professional Web design company
and individual.

American Special Interest Group on Hypertext, Hypermedia and
the Web (SIGWEB)
www.sigweb.org
SIGWEB welcomes members concerned with the World Wide Web
as well as those concerned with other aspects of hypertext and hypermedia. Offers a wealth of publications, conferences, and resource
archives covering a broad spectrum of technical expertise and providing first-hand knowledge of the latest development trends.

Writing

iUniverse.com Publishing Company
www.iUniverse.com
Helps individuals publish, market, and sell their books using print on demand service (POD). Has more than 12,000 titles in its backlist and publishes 400 new fiction and nonfiction titles each month.

The Writer's Market
www.writersmarket.com
The freelance writer's "bible" for getting published. Provides the most complete market information available, but also tips for getting published, professional advice from top agents and editors, formatting information, and much more. Available online in an expanded, easy-to-use, always up-to-date format.

www.writerswrite.com
Links to reference resources including dictionaries, encyclopedias, government agencies, and science and health Web sites that writers might want to visit. Additional information on writers' conferences, job listings, and media-industry news.

Society for Technical Communication
www.stc.org
Individual membership organization dedicated to advancing the arts and sciences of technical communication. Its 25,000 members include technical writers and editors, content developers, documentation specialists, technical illustrators, instructional designers, academics, information architects, visual designers, Web designers and developers, and translators.

www.featurewell.com
An electronic marketplace for the global publishing industry. This Web site provides editors with the opportunity to purchase and republish top-quality journalism.

Writing-World.com
http://writing-world.com
Features a collection of articles about writing query letters, freelancing, selling your work internationally, self-publishing, and promoting yourself.

Yoga

Yoga Alliance
www.yogaalliance.org
Registry for yoga teachers and schools who demonstrate qualifications that meet minimum teaching standards.

Kripalu
www.kripalu.org
A spiritual retreat and program center serving people of all backgrounds for more than twenty years. Kripalu was founded on the yogic philosophy that physical health is the foundation of mental and spiritual development. The center offers a wide range of yoga, self-discovery, holistic health, and spiritual programs. It is located in the heart of the scenic Berkshires, near Tanglewood, in Massachusetts.

International Yoga Teachers Association
www.iyta.org.au
Established in 1967 in Sydney, Australia, the International Yoga Teachers Association has members, representatives, or established branches in twenty-nine countries around the world. International Yoga Conferences are held approximately every three years in different countries around the world.

Iyengar Yoga
www.bksiyengar.com
Committed to the dissemination and promotion of the art, science, and philosophy of yoga according to the teachings of B. K. S. Iyengar and his family. Site includes a directory of Iyengar yoga teachers and regional associations.

Kundalini
www.3ho.org
Founded by Yogi Bhajan in 1969, the 3HO Foundation revolves around the simple belief that to be healthy, happy, and holy is the essence of a fulfilled life. The focus is on kundalini yoga, as taught by Yogi Bhajan, who is credited with bringing kundalini teaching to the West.

Magazines

Yoga International
www.yimag.org

Yoga Journal
www.yogajournal.com

Index

V

VC. *See* Venture capital (VC)
  industry
Vega, Yvette, 152
Venture capital (VC) industry,
  56–58
Video game designers, 176
Vila, Bob, 188–89
Vision, keeping, 23–25
Visual managers, 174
Visual merchandisers, 176
Voiceover artists, 177
von Bidder, Alex, 68

W

Wardrobe stylists, 177
Wartell, Warren, 133–34
Water, drinking, 120
Web designers, 178
Web sites. *See* Resources
Weintraub, Michael, 74
Wekselbaum, Natan, 189

Wells-Ware, 3
Williams, Mary Jane, 80
Wilson, Tina, 22
Win-win situations, 114
Wolf, Doug, 166
Women
  entrepreneurs, 39
  motherhood, family, work and,
    81–85
Work addiction. *See* Burnout
  avoidance
Workaholics. *See* Burnout
  avoidance
Work/life programs, 74–75
Workplace design, 45
Writing articles, 111

Y

Yamaguchi, Jeffrey, 26, 129

Z

Zarem, Bobby, 190